Beyond Religion

Beyond Religion

MEDITATIONS ON MAN'S TRUE NATURE

THE VISION OF ROBERT POWELL:

Selected Essays, Reflections, and Public Talks from 1970 to 2000

BLUE DOVE PRESS
SAN DIEGO • CALIFORNIA • 2001

The mission of the Blue Dove Foundation is to deepen the spiritual life of all by making available works on the lives, messages and examples of saints and sages of all religions and traditions as well as other spiritual titles that provide tools for inner growth.

For a free catalog, contact:
The Blue Dove Foundation
4204 Sorrento Valley Blvd., Suite K
San Diego, CA 92121
Phone: (858) 623-3330
website: www.bluedove.org E-mail: bdp@bluedove.org

FIRST EDITION

Cover design: Wendi Hall, Tracy Dezenzo and Sandy Shaw
Text design: Tracy Dezenzo and Sandy Shaw
Copy editor: Mary Kowit

Special thanks to Nathalie Brown for her patience and skill in the production of this work

ISBN: 1-884997-31-7
Printed in Canada

Library Cataloging-in-Publication Data:
Powell, Robert, 1918-
Beyond religion : meditations on our true nature: the vision of Robert Powell : selected essays, reflections, and public talks, 1970-2000.--1st ed.
    p. cm.
ISBN 1-884997-31-7 (pbk.)
  1.Spiritual life. 2. Spiritual life--Hinduism.
  3.Meditations I. Title
BL624 .p6697 2000
291.2--dc21   00-046805

ABOUT THE AUTHOR

Robert Powell was born in Amsterdam, The Netherlands, in 1918. After obtaining his doctorate in chemistry from London University, he pursued his career first as an industrial chemist and later as a science writer and editor, in Britain and the United States. In 1968 and 1969, he published nine chemical engineering monographs still in use by academic and industrial libraries throughout the world.

Robert Powell's personal exploration of spirituality began in the 1960's, and his quest for self-discovery led him to Zen and a number of spiritual masters, including J. Krishnamurti and Ramana Maharshi. His own spiritual awakening coincided with his discovery of the teachings of Sri Nisargadatta Maharaj. He is the editor of a Nisargadatta trilogy, also published by Blue Dove, and the author of a number of books on what he describes as "human consciousness transformation." Powell now lives a busy life in La Jolla, California, with his loving wife Gina.

ACKNOWLEDGMENTS

"The Arrival of the Third Millennium and the Illusion of Time" formed a chapter in the book *Voices on the Threshold of Tomorrow — 145 Views of the New Millennium*, edited by Georg Feuerstein and Trisha Lamb Feuerstein, published by Quest Books, 1993.

"Awareness in the Teachings of J. Krishnamurti and Sri Ramana Maharshi" was first published in *The Mountain Path*, June 1991, page 58.

"*Maya* Can Never Embrace Brahman" was first published in *The Mountain Path*, January 1991, page 174.

"Ending Misery by Unhooking from the Limited" was first published in *The Mountain Path*, December 1991, page 171.

CONTENTS

INTRODUCTION

What are "meditations"? A meditation "takes place" when I look at an object or situation without the slightest foreknowledge, as though I truly see it for the first time. In Zen they use an expression called "Beginner's mind," which sums up rather well what I mean in this connection by looking without foreknowledge, with a fresh, unsullied mind.

A meditation is different from contemplation, which is looking with the aid of existing knowledge, usually within the framework of collective, societal thought. Numerous meditations are possible and helpful, but there is only one of supreme importance; it is the meditation on the theme "Who am I?" This leads eventually to the recognition that one is the Unicity, the Totality or the Consciousness Itself, beyond all limitations and divisions. Meditation is hard work, but necessary. It essentially consists in eternal watchfulness, the witnessing of the consciousness everlastingly falling back into seeing events as variations on the theme of body-mind identification. If we don't succeed at once, we should try again. This applies to all of us, no matter how advanced our spiritual development may be. It took Sri Nisargadatta Maharaj three years after transmittal of the basics, the essential "what's what," from his own guru. It is a matter of continuously dispelling the darkness, so that there may be light. It is not for nothing that the original meaning of the term "guru" is "dispeller of darkness," the darkness here being purely ignorance of our own nature.

Reintroducing the Miraculous

No, I don't mean the miraculous aspect of science, which is certainly there. I mean the *truly* miraculous, the truly inexplicable, that which totally transcends space-time and the intellect, the realization of the *advaitic* world view or the Self, which makes *everything* miraculous. There is something which terminates all explanations, all conventional assumptions that the brain can summon. For it goes directly to the root cause of our world view, the make-up of the intellect which fabricates all explanations, all views of ourselves and the world.

The miraculous takes place when we return to the Source, the source of our Being which we discover is at once the source of everything. That source is no different from our Self, can only be our Self.

—*Robert Powell*

Beyond Religion

*We are so used to seeing things in the mirror
of time, but that mirror is a distorting one.
Only seeing things from the Emptiness,
which is the timeless or the eternal,
brings a true vision of reality.*

~ Robert Powell

PART ONE

ESSAYS

Chapter One

The Arrival of the Third Millennium — A Critical Examination of the Notion of Time

To this writer, the significance of the impending advent of the third millennium lies in the opportunity it affords to reflect upon the utter insignificance of this coming and the extreme superficiality in which we function. Our lives are totally cluttered up with inessentials, since we have lost the art of living in the essential. What could be more meaningless to our well-being than the position of the calendar? And which calendar do we choose? What about the Chinese, the Muslim and the Jewish calendars? Am I supposed to believe in numerology? And if there lies any significance in the third millennium, what fundamental change then should occur at the end of 1999 when entering the next millennium? Or are my numbers all wrong and should I have picked the years 2000 and 2001 to define the transition from second to third millennium?

This attitude seems akin to the increasingly popular "thinking in terms of decades," the way we assign magical potency to periods of ten years, as though the decades themselves could exert a certain control over the affairs of man. The fifties, the sixties, the seventies, etc., each is supposed to have brought with it a certain climate of social change, a different outlook on life. If one blames the present decade for current dissatisfaction, then there remains nothing but to wait for the next one. And if one's decade has only just started, that is just too bad; then one is out of luck and must be patient for the numbers to change. Thus, man in the absence of real understanding of himself stays entangled in all kinds of number games, which are nothing but rank superstition.

What do we mean by "change"? For myself, all change is a delusion. Only unreal things change. The real is that which never changes and alone therefore can be said to have identity. We think in terms of change, because our thinking is pervaded with the notion of time. That is why even the deepest thinking is inherently superficial, as it is based on the notion that there is progression. But that progression is only conceptual, not actual. The French say: "*Plus ça change, plus c'est la même chose*," but even this saying is predicated upon the notion of time. I am hinting at something much more fundamental, which should be explored in depth because this very notion holds a powerful key to self-discovery. And if there is such a thing as a direct path to self-realization, it might well be the understanding of this question.

We talk about the past and the future, but where are they? What are they? Can anyone produce a sample of the past or the future? Has anyone ever been able to do anything to the past, to "undo" the past? If one thinks so, one is doing it in the present and to the present. Has anyone ever been able to manipulate the future? If one thinks so, then think again for one is doing it in the present. We can never escape from the present moment; it is all that ever is. The past is just one kind of image, a memory, and (projecting) the future is another kind of "imaging" or imagination — both produced by thought. The present moment is all that exists, and it is timeless and limitless. What does this timeless moment consist of? Nothing but Awareness; not awareness of something but pure Sentience, what has also been referred to as the state of "I am." It is the only state that one can rightly claim as one's own. Every other state — I am "this" or I am "that" introduces concept, thought, and is therefore disputable. Anything else that one "owns" is predicated upon this quality of Awareness for without it there can be no knowledge of ownership or of anything else.

J. Krishnamurti has stated that there is chronological time and psychological time and that for him only the first exists. My position is more extreme; it is that not even chronological time exists — a truth which has been held by all the *advaitic* masters. There is nothing but the present moment, and it is not simply that man is ever in the present, he verily *is* the present moment; he is pure Presence or Awareness and is all that ever exists. That is why Sri Nisargadatta Maharaj was able to declare: "Nobody existed prior to me" (in *The Ultimate Medicine*, Blue Dove Press, San Diego, 1995).

It is this split in the indivisible that has proved so disastrous, because it leads to the birth of an imaginary entity, the "me," that sets off a lifelong concern for its well-being with a concomitant drain of energy. All this is the play of *Maya*. In reality there is neither birth nor death; there is only Awareness or Consciousness. Neither body nor mind really exists other than as composites of sensory impressions — superimpositions on that Consciousness. Just as a movie is projected as a play of light and dark on a blank screen, so the entire manifest reality comes onto the Awareness as pure appearance during the waking and dream states. In the deep sleep state, *Maya* is held in abeyance: the projector is turned off.

Does the statement that time does not really exist mean that I should throw away my watch and calendar? Of course not, unless I decide to become a renunciant. I would no longer be able to function in a society that lives rigidly by those yardsticks. But that does not necessarily mean that they are real and not merely empirical. As far as the mind is concerned, time is real but the mind is not the final arbiter in these things. On the contrary, since the mind itself is of the nature of conceptual time — it has come about through identification of consciousness with a particular body and name — whatever it perceives is tainted by those limitations.

Here lies at once a clue to humanity's unhappiness and possible release. Living in an unreal time dimension, at every moment of one's existence there is a certain expectancy regarding the next moment: this causes a dimming of our attention to the Present since thought hopes for the next moment to be better or, alternatively, fears it to be worse. Or if we are bored, we are looking toward the next moment for something to "happen" that will relieve our ennui. Always looking forward to the "future," we have found it very difficult to live in the fullness of what *is*; thus, a peculiar quality is brought about in the consciousness, which is experienced as the "flow of time" and on a deeper level, as the energy of "becoming," which is the seed of all misery *(samsara)*. We are constantly in the grip of desire — a desire for a change in our condition — and so are never free. Only in rare moments, in the intervals between (the satisfaction of) consecutive desires and in the deep-sleep state, when there is pure Being or Presence without any mind activity, do we get a foretaste of the blissful state that is our birthright since it is our real nature. There is no notion of change and the mind is totally still: Nothing exists in that silence but the pure state of Awareness with its inherent blissfulness *(ananda)*.

Can it perhaps now be seen why spiritual practices that comprise a conscious effort to be free of *samsara* must be self-defeating because they keep the mind from being still and beget more time? Paradoxically, it may be stated therefore that the most difficult practice is to abstain from all practice! The very idea that we are in bondage immediately produces an impulse to break free, but that very movement toward the projected freedom is the bondage, because it is again an escape from the present and therefore still part of our habitual "becoming." So what is needed only is the perception that there is no bondage, that we are free here and now. Thus, the direct path is to persuade the mind that it can totally relax, which is only another way of stating the need for its total surrender. This leads to a condition which combines the best features of both the sleep and waking states; Ramana Maharshi called it *jagrat-sushupti,* or wakeful sleep. It may also be called sleepless waking, the culmination of perfect awareness and perfect stillness.

Chapter Two

Awareness in the Teachings of J. Krishnamurti and Sri Ramana Maharshi

J. Krishnamurti talks a great deal about "choiceless awareness" — it may well be regarded as the mainstay of his teaching — yet people have great difficulty with it. One of the questions asked again and again by his students is: "If awareness is choiceless, then who is it that is aware?" Now, first of all, in phrasing it this way, are we not begging the question? The grammatical structure of the sentence implies that there be a subject corresponding to the verb, in this case, an entity who is aware. Because language reflects our thinking patterns, the implication is normally justified. But where it concerns truly fundamental questions, we cannot always be sure that the semantics are

9

a reliable guide to comprehension. (It is not unlike situations in modern physics, where the language of mathematics does not always yield insight into the real nature of fundamental particles or events.)

To go into this question more fully, let me take the example of looking at a mountain. I ask myself: "Is there an observer who is engaged in observing the mountain, or does there take place an autonomous, natural process without duality — that is, without conscious effort on the part of the observer?" I maintain that if there is complete attention to the mountain, which means that one looks at it non-geologically or in total silence, there is only that mountain and no observer whatsoever — which does not mean that the observer has become the mountain! The observer comes into being only when, for example, one starts looking at the mountain geologically, that is, with one's knowledge and experience of mountains, saying: "What a lovely mountain!" or, "It is frightfully barren," "It is a volcano," and so on.

Normally, we look analytically, with a specialized eye, from the background of our knowledge and experience, and therefore in a partial or fragmented way. The initially pure perception is immediately cut short by the analytical mind, which introduces a comparative, evaluative element in the observation and thus creates the "observer." Furthermore, perception is usually accompanied by either pleasure or pain; and the desire to perpetuate pleasure and avoid pain adds a new dimension to the observer; it imposes a psychological superstructure on the observer.

Thus, we might say that choiceless awareness, in which there isn't an entity that is aware, entails looking at an object without thought. In the above example, it would mean looking at a mountain in the same way that one looks at a flat piece of ground. (Could this perhaps be the meaning of that old Chinese saying:"When I began to study Zen, mountains were mountains; when I thought I understood Zen, mountains were not mountains; but when I came to full knowledge of Zen, mountains were again mountains"?[1] If I can look in this way, and not only at mountains, but also at a woman, a man, a child — at everything around me — as well as all that which goes on psychologically within my skin, then I shall find that I no longer nurture a center of conditioning and strengthen the subconscious.

For example, when I observe in myself greed, violence and sensuality, the mind affixes the appropriate labels and sets in motion the whole comparative, evaluative process of thought which has been conditioned by morality to condemn or approve the thought or the action. Consequently, the mind might then endeavor to attain the ideal of non-greed, non-violence, non-sensuality, little by little, on the assumption that if sufficient effort is made over a long enough period, eventually the mind will be "purified." Thus, the psychological fact — my actual condition, which is the Unknown because we never come into direct contact with it — is ever reduced to the known, a concept projected by thought.

Now Krishnamurti maintains that if we can look with complete attention, without naming, comparing, and so on — all of which constitutes the mind's habitual reaction — the Unknown will reveal its significance to us and it will be possible to go beyond both greed and non-greed, violence and non-violence, not in due course but immediately.

This is so, he states, because at no time has there been an observer who is greedy or violent, but merely a psychological state, a particular "feeling," which has only momentary existence. When we create duality with the "observer"

---

[1] Attributed to Ch'ing Yuan, as quoted by Professor D.T. Suzuki in *The Role of Nature in Zen Buddhism, Studies of Zen*, Rider, London, 1957, p.187.

who reacts to his condition by naming it "greed," "violence," and the like, we perpetuate that momentary state by triggering a tug-of-war between greed and non-greed, a play of the opposites that has no end. In other words, when we try to become virtuous in the traditional, moral sense by "self-improvement," there is nothing in store for us but bondage. But when the self is transcended in the actual process of self-knowing, there is an immediate freedom which is not a reaction to bondage.

Let us now consider Sri Ramana Maharshi's teaching. He views both the observer and the object as unreal, mere reflections of the eternal Self, which alone is real. On waking, both appear simultaneously, similar in manner to the (mutually dependent) origination of the "I" and the "world" in a dream. With the onset of deep sleep, both disappear again. At first glance, this might seem contradictory to the mechanism described above, especially Krishnamurti's contention that there *is* an observer even though this entity can be dissolved in a state of awareness. On closer examination, however, it will be seen that Krishnamurti's and Maharshi's views about phenomenal existence do not contradict each other but actually converge.

First of all, it must be recognized that the teachings appear to differ because they employ — or rather, imply — different definitions of the "observer" and the "object." To Maharshi, all "things" are only reflections of the one Reality and as such have no existence of their own. Thus, the "observer" and the "object," in the intervals during which they manifest themselves, have only a borrowed existence. They are creations of the mind, which is the manifestation of the "I" and secures its continuity through giving reality to name and form. Krishnamurti is primarily interested in the "observer" as a *psychological* entity. When he speaks of the "observer," it is in this sense only, since his whole teaching is essentially psychological in nature. Maharshi, on the other hand, treats the observer as a total entity (psyche+soma), which he calls the ego or the "I." He further deals with the relationship, if relationship be the right word, of this finite ego to the infinite matrix or Source, which he calls the Self and sometimes refers to as "I-I."

Krishnamurti takes the physical reality of both observer and object for granted; or perhaps more accurately, he does not question their physical existence and refuses to be drawn into speculation on their ultimate nature. Since he is not concerned with erecting a new system of philosophy or creating an all-embracing *Weltanschauung*, this type of questioning is immaterial to him. Furthermore, dealing only with the practical aspects of living, Krishnamurti probably feels that to burden his teaching with ontological and metaphysical issues would only distract from his main message and likely confuse his listener. And, anyway, that the clue to the problem of Being is divulged best through self-knowing, thus rendering any intellectual discourse on such matters superfluous. In this connection, his attitude appears similar to that of the Zen Masters.

In Maharshi's teaching, due to its different character, or rather, its different approach and viewpoint, these considerations do not apply. This is because an examination of the nature of physical reality forms an integral and essential part of his teaching from its inception. Through directly inquiring into the question "Who am I?", and immediately following through on any further question(s), such as "Who is it that is trying to figure out this fundamental question?" (possibly in an infinite regress!), one bypasses all intellectual and metaphysical probing. On pursuing this process of inquiry *(vichara)* vigorously, the mind exhausts itself, returns whence it came, and the thought flow comes to an end. In other words, the befuddling power of thought activity is stilled most effectively right from the start. The mind, which is normally considered as the only means to solve a problem, is exposed as ineffectual because it is seen to constitute the very problem itself!

Thus, any apparent contradiction between the two teachings is due to the fact that we are confusing psychological and physical levels and different points of view in the description of man and the world. To Krishnamurti, the ego is born from moment to moment with the state of inattention (duality), but it is possible — by being totally aware in the manner described — not to nurture the desire-activated and desire-bound entity, which he calls the "observer." When the observer as a psychological entity has been transcended in this manner, he remains as a physical entity, but this, falling outside the scope of Krishnamurti's interest, is not considered any further. As Krishnamurti does not adhere to the concept of *Maya*, there is only one level of reality to him, and the very fact of an object's physicality confirms its objective existence.

As already stated, in Maharshi's teaching, the observer has empirical existence for intermittent periods and comes into being with the arising of the "I-thought," which has emerged from the real and eternal Self. This "I"- consciousness then identifies with the body, and for a period the entire world manifests as separate entities possessed of name and form. All that disappears with the onset of deep sleep, when the "I"- thought returns into the Self.

Krishnamurti's teaching, if I may put it somewhat crudely, partly overlaps Maharshi's. He describes the primary non-psychological component of the observing faculty very clearly as the formation of a "center of recognition" entailing the following sequence: perception, memory, and naming. Functioning as we do, and communicating in duality or relativity, this kind of observer has a necessary life of its own and does not in itself lead to bondage. But with the arising of desire, in our usual state of nescience, bondage comes into being.

However, in the state of awareness as pointed to by Krishnamurti, desire remains a momentary experience in the nature of pure "feeling-energy." And, most importantly, since it is not named or acted upon in any way, it is no longer given continuity. Consequently, the psychological counterpart of the observing entity is never born. Psychological time, with its fears, conflicts, anxieties and prevailing moods of sadness, is never given a chance to take hold, and one truly lives from moment to moment. (The mountain is once again seen as a mountain, yet the quality of seeing has radically changed. At first, when the mountain was perceived, it was simply "seeing." Then the action became "non-seeing," and finally, it comprises both "seeing" and "non-seeing.")

Maharshi admonishes us to pursue without letup the inquiries "Who am I?," "To whom is this happening?," and so on, not because there is such a "who" but because in the very search we shall discover its unreality — and this discovery puts an immediate end to the prevailing ego-sense. Since the observer as a psychological entity is nothing but a stream of thoughts, activated and maintained by desire, it can be readily seen that an examination of what is happening to that entity by pursuing the inquiry "Who am I?" must be essentially the same as the process of self-knowing in choiceless awareness. Both teachings have as common denominator the injunction: "Find out who is the observer, then see what happens."

Finally, regarding the "practice" of awareness as a spiritual discipline or exercise at regular times, we might ask, "Who is it that is practicing awareness?" If it is done through special effort, as an exertion of "Will," and I say to myself, "I am going to listen to what my mind tells me," then I have created the "listener" or the "observer," and therefore duality, which excludes choiceless awareness. True meditation does not allow for any feedback. If you are conscious that you are listening to music, then you are not all-listening. Similarly, if you are consciously engaged in being aware, then you are *not* aware; you are striving to be aware, you are still part of a process of "becoming" and so in a state of subtle conflict or duality.

We must point out here, however, that the term "awareness" means different things to Krishnamurti and Maharshi. In the former's teaching, awareness is the sense of "I-am-ness," the Beingness or Universal Consciousness, resulting from transcendence of the psychological observer or the "I." To Maharshi, awareness is identical with the Self or the Absolute, which is realized when, in turn, the "I-am-ness" or Universal Consciousness is transcended. Because this awareness or the Absolute has spawned the entire relative world, it cannot logically be defined in terms of those relative things — space-time, matter and mind — being totally beyond the grasp of the intellect. Hence, it is sometimes referred to simply as That (the famous expression "That Thou Art" equates our identity with it). And it has been "defined" in the only possible manner as "I Am That I Am," a self-contained or circular definition, since the highest truth can obviously never be defined in terms of lower truths.

Once Maharshi was asked how to obtain and cultivate awareness. He answered: "You are awareness. Awareness is another name for you. All that you have to do is to give up being aware of other things; that is, of the not-Self. If one gives up being aware of them, then pure awareness alone remains, and that is the Self.[2] In this con-

2 A. Devaraja Mudaliar, *Day By Day With Bhagavan*, p.244.

nection, "other things" can only mean "all the things of this world," since the Self is not one of them but is actually their ultimate Source.

It may thus be clear that what constitutes one's training ground for *sadhana* comprises the whole of everyday living, which includes minor matters as well as the most testing situations, and not only when the mind is "under observation" and therefore on its best behavior. True spirituality requires constant vigilance, a witnessing of all one's actions and relationships, so that one does not get caught in any of the "other things" Maharshi refers to. After all, why stay awake only part of the day? Why let inattention create more problems than necessary? If one sees the urgency of the matter, every moment counts. Then one will naturally live every day as though it were one's last.

Chapter Three

Maya Can Never Embrace Brahman

One of our main problems is that we find it nearly impossible to reconcile the insights of the Upanishads and their more recent proponents, the *Advaita Vedanta* masters, with our actual, everyday-life experience. And, I feel, this might well be the only problem from which all other problems derive. The teachings state that everything is really one Whole (non-dual), that there are no individual entities such as "you" and "me," and that any differences we perceive are illusory. In fact, the entire manifest world is *Maya* (illusory); the Unmanifest or the Noumenon only is real but, as indicated by the definition of these terms, "unknowable." Thus, since there are no differences, there is nothing to strive for, not even realization since we are the Real already. We must just stop "pretending" we are not That (the Real) — something we have done for so long that in the end we have hypnotized ourselves into believing in our own ignorance. Thus, all we need to do to is to wake up from our dream state and be true to our (non-dual) Self.

Such an attitude to life runs completely counter to our everyday experience of a tangible world, in which we are highly conscious of our separate self-identities, and of the differences between one individual and another. After all, it is these differences that underlie the motivation for all action on the psychological level — to "better ourselves," and, ultimately, "survive" as that independent entity, the "me."

So our difficulty is: How do we deal with this antithesis of diametrically opposite world views, especially when one of these is based on actual life experience and the other, to us, from hearsay? Here it must first be pointed out that all experience is based on the senses, and these often deceive us. For centuries man believed that the sun revolves around the earth, since it had been our daily experience that the sun rises and sets on a stationary earth, which was considered to be the center of the Universe. When, subsequently, the knowledge of our solar system began to broaden, man began to realize the error of his world-view and the limits of intuitive perception.

However, worse was to come with the findings of the so-called "new physics," which allowed even less scope for intuitive perception or comprehension. As examples, we might mention the concept of light being both particles and waves, and "matter" being a curvature of space. Those concepts are not only wholly alien to our intuition but are also in direct contradiction to common sense and even beyond the reach of linear thought.

In the spiritual area, the great masters of all wisdom traditions have always challenged deeply rooted assumptions and habitual ways of perceiving and conceptualizing. They never tired of pointing out certain undeniable facts, generally unrealized because of being contrary to intuitive perception, which may bring one closer to an understanding of *advaita* or non-duality. To some aspirants, such pointers have proved extremely helpful, in their role of "hints," although falling short of providing definite "proof," if there be such a thing; to others, possibly less advanced, they seem to have merely added to the confusion in their minds. Now I do not think one can ever produce an absolute proof for the truth of *advaita* as one does with a mathematical or scientific proposition. And even if such a "proof" were to be forthcoming, it would still be on the intellectual plane and not be transcendental apperception or realization leading to the liberation of consciousness. I do not believe the latter can be communicated from one person to another, and I will later state why.

One such hint that the *advaita* masters have given us is that, were it not for identification with the body, the idea of being a separate individual would not have arisen; in fact, such a concept simply could not be. From this the following ensues logically: in the absence of an observer, distinct in space and time, there are no objects distinct in space and time. In other words, if the observer sees himself as a separate entity, then the world appears before him as separate entities. And if the observer regards himself as the Totality, then the world is similarly observed — as one indivisible Whole. Another way to understand this is to state that since fundamentally the observer is the observed, both must be of a like nature.

Now some persons on hearing that the mind is wrongly identified with the body will interpret *advaita* by positing that a multiplicity of bodies exist as separate entities, but that psychologically we are one; that is, our minds are not separate but one. This, roughly speaking, has been Krishnamurti's essential point of view and teaching. (K never accepted the concept of *Maya*.) But such a world-view brings with it its own difficulties, since it primarily retains and strengthens the false split between body and mind. For if our bodies exist as multiple entities and the mind as a unicity, they must necessarily be of fundamentally different natures and then we have only reasserted the false duality of body-mind or matter-consciousness. Another possible consequence is that the mind starts to rationalize and project various concepts, such as by saying to itself: "All these separate minds are empowered by one energy; I am energy and so feel myself as being part of the universal energy," which is merely another explanation, a purely intellectual one, for that matter, and ultimately meaningless: it does not touch me in the core of my being and I still have not reached *advaita*.[1]

My view is that explanations of any kind do not really help us much in understanding our own nature; in a sense, they hold us back from a total, direct realization. This is because any form of explanation entails concepts, and concepts necessarily maintain the momentum of the intellectual process. And, more to the point, explanations refer only to *Maya*; therefore, for *Maya* to end, explanations must come to an end. And, while insights can and must be shared, the magic of such a transfer takes place more often through silence than anything else. For ultimately, it is impossible to make anyone see a spiritual truth through ratiocination or intellectual persuasion, or to transport another person to one's own state of bliss. To quote Ramana Maharshi: "Thoughts must cease and reason disap-

---

1 In this connection, Sri Ramana Maharshi stated: "All that you see depends on the seer. Apart from the seer, there is no seen." — A. Devaraja Mudaliar, *Day by Day with Bhagavan*, p.149; and "Without the seer there are no objects seen." — *Talks with Sri Ramana Maharshi*, First American Edition, Inner Directions Foundation, Carlsbad, 2000.

pear for 'I-I' to rise up and be felt. Feeling is the prime factor and not reason."[2] (By "I-I" Ramana refers to the true Self
or Brahman.) Also relevant is a remark by Sri Nisargadatta
Maharaj to the effect that "your facts may be imagination to
me, and my facts may be imagination to you." Thus, explanations can, at best, hint at the truth but can never prove or
convey that truth to another. Truth must be realized by oneself for oneself. Thus, the real utility of explanations may
well lie in silencing the mind through showing its impotence, and thereby prepare a condition or susceptibility for
Grace to operate. For realization is essentially acausal: it can
be neither induced nor impeded. And, in last resort, everything is Grace.

There is another, much more compelling reason why
the truth of *advaita* — our self-nature — cannot be formulated and thereby "known" in any way. The very process
of "knowing," our entire intellectual-emotional cognitive
activity, takes place strictly in and as the realm of *Maya*; it
is a *Mayaic* activity. The seeker himself is nothing but
Maya, and this seeker wants to establish the truth about
the non-dual — that is, the pure, objectless, attributeless
consciousness which is called Brahman.

The important thing to see is that whatever that body-
mind entity concludes can only describe how things
appear to that empirical entity which finds its being in the
realm of *Maya*. And, as we have already seen, since the
observer is the observed, the body-mind entity can only
find out and make statements about *Maya*, never about
Brahman. A fragment can only describe the fragmentary,
the finite can only define the finite, never the infinite. To
use a simple analogy, a water droplet thrown up in the
foam above the ocean surface theoretically could say some-

---

[2] Ibid., p. 17.

thing about itself, since it has borders; that is, it interfaces with a milieu other than itself. But the same droplet as part of the body of the ocean could do no such thing; it cannot know itself, in the traditional meaning of the term. Where is the "droplet" and where is the ocean? It would be the Wholeness, beyond any subject-object relationship. Just so, we must view our psychosomatic being, our falsely assumed and experienced "ego"; it is no other than the ocean of Consciousness, beyond space-time, beyond knowing and not-knowing, beyond existing and not-existing. Such realization can only take place when the mental process has been silenced, and knowledge as cognition is transcended.

Chapter Four

Ending Misery by Unhooking from the Limited

    I find myself in my present position — that of limitation, vulnerability, inevitably leading to suffering — due to the presence of a multitude of frames of reference within which I function. These "hooks," of psychological origin, restrict my freedom and spell conflict; yet, they are wholly of my own making, and can therefore be undone or made ineffective only by myself, and not through any outside agency. For this, it is important to recognize that the "hooks" consist entirely of "memory." The realization that they are not concrete and necessarily enduring but essentially evanescent memories, the past, signifies at once the possibility of their dissolution. Thus, contrary to the prevalent notion that the limits to our freedom are the results of external factors, the truth is that our restraints are, in fact, internal, self-constructed from concepts and habits of thought. They endure only because they are so rarely examined and exposed for what they are.

The hooks in question are the multitude of commitments and entanglements entered into willingly and sometimes not so willingly in the course of a lifetime. (But even where they have come about under pressure from others, ultimately, they are our responsibility, because we have acceded to their imposition.) Liberation is to be effected only by dissolving the hooks of memory by means of the universal solvent of awareness. In observing the nature of the "hooks" in detail, we find they are the attitudes, inclinations, unfulfilled desires, psychological commitments, etc. (collectively called *vasanas* in Hindu literature) that form the unexamined portion of our consciousness or the Unconscious. In their totality, they make up the basis of what is called our "individuality" or "personality." Were it not for this aggregate of *vasanas*, there would be nothing static, only a smoothly flowing stream of thoughts. Although we call it "mind," when completely fluid it is actually No-Mind, since it concerns only an abstraction; there are no conflicts and it causes no problems.

It is further important to understand that when we talk of "hooks" there is nothing that is "being hooked," because the hooks in their totality are at once the unreal entity that is in bondage. Thus, the *vasanas* — our antecedents, frames of reference vis-à-vis other persons, ideas, and habitual activities, all the social roles we act out — are the elements that maintain our limitation and so long as they prevail, our unhappiness will endure. Can we perhaps already see which way freedom beckons?

So the question then is: How to undo the hooks without in the process bringing about new ones? No conscious action on my part can be the answer, because any such action would ultimately be the work of the very hooks that are the problem. It is enough to expose the hooks, which are my shackles, to the light of attention, moving them from the unconscious past into the conscious present. It is most important to see their temporal nature; that is, they have entered at a certain point in time by slipping in, as it were, through my lack of awareness, and henceforth have steadfastly strengthened themselves.

Another way to visualize our situation is to realize that, contents-wise, the flow of thoughts representing our mental activity is not completely random, as it *appears* to be. If it were, there would be no problems, as no conflict and no bondage would arise. But there is a certain polarization of the thought-content which gives rise to tension within the field of thought; that is, thoughts are essentially self-oriented or self-centered, and by "self" we mean the empirical center that has come about through identification with a particular body. The latter immediately creates a location in space, where one appears to find oneself. Also, a time-span is created in which one appears to function, since the idea of a "beginning" comes about with the birth of the body, and that which has a beginning in time must necessarily have an ending. This empirical "self" is wholly a matter of images and concepts, all based on memory. By this we mean that it gives rise to a situation as if there were an entity and as if there were a world, or an entity who could get something out of that world and/or fear the world as a threat to its security.

When this polarization is cancelled, there is an essentially random flow of thought. Then, the remaining non-randomness of thought is no longer self-centered and the breeding ground of conflict but has become problem-centered and creative, when by "problem" we mean that which at any particular moment happens to appear in the focus of attention, our disinterested interest or scientific curiosity, and immune to the fields of desire and fear. Even though the thought patterns are "meaningful" and therefore non-random within the scope of any one particular "problem," within a wider area the flow is random as it is no longer guided or controlled by an all-overriding pattern of "self"-interest. Thus, this randomization is the liberating factor, since it enables one to forget "oneself" and act without the scourge of self-consciousness.

How and when does this condition come about? By being prior to it, when one sees clearly how one has got into a particular thought structure, how one has adopted a particular mind-set in the course of time — and this act of perception is at once the stepping out of it — one exits from the dimension of time and enters into the timeless. It is also realized at that moment that this is all that one can do. For, basically, there are only two ways open to man, as far as his mental life is concerned. Either one aims at disciplining the mind by forcing its contents to fit into a particular conceptual mold (an overall, compelling frame of reference) or one utilizes the mind's capacity to watch its own activities. J. Krishnamurti has exposed the first possibility as being fallacious, by showing that that which makes the effort is at once that which is being worked upon, or the thinker is his thought, the observer is the observed. All such efforts are exercises in self-delusion, which Zen Master Bankei compared with washing off blood with blood. The only alternative is letting activities go on unhindered, but carefully watching all the thoughts — which is a much more difficult thing than it seems.

Thus, the two fundamental approaches in the current situation signify that one either goes along lazily with the various binding thought-flow patterns and struggles reflexively with their various components — our normal way of functioning — or one *merely* witnesses them and thereby steps resolutely out of them. If one should do this, which is really a "non-doing" because it is primarily watching without interference with whatever is observed, then the moment will come when this "me" is wholly the witness. One is completely detached from any action and from any "doer" who then may be a totally separate entity. One is the background upon which everything happens, or as Nisargadatta Maharaj would express it: one is what one was one year before one's birth. By looking at my thought processes in this way, I come to realize the condition before the various frames of reference came into being and got hold of me (that is, disrupted the smooth-flowing thought stream). All the seeds of conflict, the many subtle identifications, reveal themselves spontaneously without the "me" working upon them or indeed having anything to do with the process. For it is a natural law that tension within the consciousness ever strives to relieve itself if one opens oneself up sufficiently: consciousness as the flow of thoughts naturally tends towards the non-random state. Finally, I arrive at the situation as I was prior to the existence of these shackles: I have totally "unhooked" myself; analogous to the operation of the Second Law of Thermodynamics on the physical plane, entropy is maximized also on the psychic plane.

In this connection, "prior to" is a most important concept; it is one of the few concepts capable of eliminating all other concepts if applied consistently to its very end. Its significance is not only time-wise, as "previous to," but also as "primordial, of a higher order of reality" — denoting the matrix or source material. For example, thought, whether in its primitive or most sophisticated form, is always reactive or reflexive, ultimately deriving from the primordial "I"-thought or the concept of duality. It appears in my sentience or consciousness, just as clouds appear in a blue sky.

Thus, consciousness is prior to thought. By the same token, the source of consciousness or the Absolute is prior to consciousness; going along this reverse sequence, one arrives at a point where conceptualization is nonexistent: concepts have yet to come into existence. Only thereafter, with consciousness, does the pain come.

Since at one time I functioned quite happily and freely without these hooks, as in fact I still do whenever I am dreamlessly asleep, I can go into reverse by mentally — and actually — going prior to my self-assumed and self-determined hooks. And, as already stated, doing so is made all that much easier upon realization that the hooks are not actually concrete and therefore lasting but are nothing more than images and concepts held in memory banks. Originally nothing but fleeting memories, they have been given a magical existence and continuity by constant recall and being acted out in relationship. This very process must be thoroughly understood. At its core lies the identification with the "body." What makes the process particularly tenacious is the fact that all thought patterns within the scope of self-orientation are essentially in aid of survival of the body, and so, by extension, the ego. Now in itself there is nothing wrong with the physical preservation of a body, but what is pernicious is the sustenance of the unreal "psychological" entity that is formed as a by-product in the identification process. To let go of the thought is therefore a direct threat to the body with which it is identified. The key to detachment and dissolution of the bondage is twofold: first, it is necessary to see the false identification with a body. Second, we should patiently witness the thought formations as soon as they come up and expose them for what they are.

Without identification with a particular body, what could be my identity and *where* could I be? Would I still have a care in the world? Identity signifies being some "thing" and finding oneself at a particular place, but if I am not a "thing," I must be "nothing." Yet, since there is a distinct sense of being present, it must follow that I am everything. And similarly, since I am nowhere in particular I must be omnipresent, or simply Presence itself. Thus, because I am the fullness and the infinitude, how can I be hurt by anything? I cannot be touched by anything, yet I touch or am immanent in everything. Being the Unmanifest, and in my essence not confined within space-time, I manifest throughout space; and since I am in the present throughout time, without limitation, I am immortal. So rather than being identified with one particular body at a particular point in time, if I insist on identification of some sort, I may more properly consider myself as being identified with all the bodies, all the creatures in the world, and throughout the entire range of time.

Now what happens when I dissolve the self-created hooks or kinks in my thought flow? The state, or rather non-state, which prevails after I have placed that which I take for "myself" prior to a particular bondage-creating situation is the same as that which prevails immediately after the satisfaction of a particular desire but before a second desire has yet arisen; it is also identical with the state of dreamless sleep.

If one persistently makes this one's *sadhana*, it will gradually connect one to the pristine purity of our original being, the state or rather non-state before contamination by experience and memory took effect. Eventually, I will find myself prior to my birth-life and have therefore also become deathless (since my being born as "someone" means only to die as such). This is the state Nisargadatta Maharaj constantly refers to as the state one was in a hundred years ago, or the state "prior to consciousness" or *nirguna* (without attributes).

There is nothing else to do and really nothing else that can be done. If one distills the essence of all established approaches to realization, then in practice this is all they boil down to. Anything else that I attempt to do would be a movement within consciousness and as long as my center is exclusively within consciousness — that is, within a subject-object relationship — I remain vulnerable to suffering. Doing this *sadhana* amounts to the wiping away of all frames of reference, which is my only salvation, for every frame of reference, however elevated or exalted, brings about dualism and therefore strengthens the mental prison. When all frames of reference have been removed, I find myself back in a state of innocence that prevailed before the thought of a psychological "I" had occurred within me.

So, through this practice I have not only unhooked myself, but I have also brought about a condition of alert understanding in which new hooks cannot solidify, for before a thought pattern can crystallize, it is seen for what it is and neutralized. In this state of infinity, all sense of doership has disappeared. Everything happens automatically and there is nothing that can fundamentally affect me, because my state of being is one of complete transparency. Whatever activities take place, they no longer hold any ultimate or absolute goals; all has become mere "entertainment" and there is no longer any dread of the outcome.

Chapter Five

Happiness is Ineffable

The via negativa towards self-realization and happiness is often questioned and criticized for its negativism, by which is meant it being "excessively" and even exclusively preoccupied with suffering, instead of positively pursuing happiness. The reason for this apparently lopsided approach is very simple. Man does not have to reach out, need not make efforts towards happiness, because his fundamental nature is just that, it is happiness itself. Were it otherwise, and man had to struggle for its attainment, it would not be true happiness, because whatever is attained can be lost again. Such a contrived happiness would be conditional upon circumstances and thus ever be a fragile and relative thing in which the individual would not be truly free but always tied to those circumstances.

There is a happiness which is not fragile and does not limit the individual, because it is absolute and unconditional. It arises as soon as the conflict in the mind is resolved; nothing else is required. The conflict in the mind merely obscures the state of bliss, which is perfect silence and ever there, deep within ourselves. Unfortunately, we do not heed it, are not even aware of its existence, due to a noisy mind which is never entirely still. So there is only one thing to do, and that is to consider, with a view to its understanding, suffering. Happiness is a by-product of something else, the elimination of suffering which comes only through self-knowing. That is why it has been said that the highest path to knowledge is this *via negativa*, and why the deepest thinkers throughout time have never admonished, "Be happy!" but instead, "Know thyself!"; never "Work diligently towards happiness!" but instead "Work diligently towards your own deliverance (i.e., from suffering)!," ever emphasizing the negative aspect of removing the obstacles to finding oneself. But before the obstacles fall away, one must make the best of them. For, as Sri Atmananda (Krishna Menon) has pointed out, obstacles should be cherished and utilized since they too point towards the Consciousness.

Happiness is not an attribute of one's individuality, it *is* one's self. Therefore one does not have to go beyond oneself, one does not need anything external. It is enough simply to find oneself.

All efforts to move towards this state in a positive way are only distractions from the only thing that matters, and therefore they are really so many steps backwards. Happiness is only come upon in a stealthy, almost incidental way, never as the result of a frontal attack upon one's unhappiness in which one is trying to approximate oneself to the projected ideal of "happiness," which is merely the opposite of one's unhappy state. Happiness is that indescribable state which lies beyond all opposites, all dualities, which is found perchance but which one cannot find.

Chapter Six

Subject and Object are Commonly Confused

J. Krishnamurti denied the existence of different levels of Reality, and one can readily agree with that, but at the same time it must be affirmed that there are different levels of understanding. And when one misses the highest level of understanding, that of *advaita* or unicity, one has not even had a taste of that Reality and lives wholly in unreality.

A good deal of our difficulty in understanding the essence of *advaita* and thereby removing the main obstacle to Self-understanding is based on a fundamental confusion between the Subjective and the Objective. We observe the material objects of this world as "objects," and in opposition to that, we make the observer, the body-mind complex, into the "subject." Incidentally, we are here not using these terms in their commonly accepted meanings of differentiating between the factual and the possibly non-factual. Quite literally, by "objective" we mean having the nature of an object or a "thing," and the "subjective" having the qualities of a perceiver, since every object needs a perceiver to warrant the title of "object," just like every North

Pole requires a South Pole for its existence.

The psychosomatic entity or ego, which is commonly held to be the universal Subject, can itself be observed like any other object even though this fact evades most of us. It is that conglomerate of concepts, thoughts and memories that has coalesced at some early stage and henceforth been developing incessantly according to its conditioning. According to Nisargadatta, once the original conceptual entity has come into existence through identification (of the consciousness) with body and name, it is at every turn fortified in its existence by exposure to further concepts; it is much like steadily driving a nail into the wall. When we examine our mental life in periods of relative quiet, we can sometimes follow the movements and shapes that the ego entity takes in its relationships with other entities, how it continuously responds to conceptualization. We can then follow the machinations of the ego, from a witnessing point of view. Then it becomes quite clear that the "I" is no less of an object than any other "thing" or object, and not the subject that we had taken it for. Nisargadatta confirms and clarifies this as follows (in *I Am That*, p. 64): "The person is never the subject. You can see a person, but you are not the person. You are always the Supreme which appears at a given point of time and space as the witness."

There is another aspect that must be noted here because it certainly is relevant. You see, the world of objects is constantly changing, and as such cannot be observed by its like, by the world of change. Only the Unchanging can observe the changeful. Therefore, it is the unchanging background only — i.e., the effulgent Consciousness — that can truly observe the changeful world, and it is this Background, which is the proper Subject that witnesses the world of objects. That is the Subject, the Self or the "I-Principle," in the words of Sri Atmananda.

Chapter Seven

Approach to Advaita from the So-Called "Object"

There is also an entirely different approach to the same end of realizing unicity. You see, we talk of "objects" as though they were established facts. But what is an "object"? Is it not a convention for an experience that is little more than an inference, or an extrapolation of a perception by the senses? I see a form, a dimension, but that form depends on my seeing, my eyes, and my brain cells to interpret the "observation." For example, what happens when I wish to differentiate whether something is a huge sphere or a tiny grain. In the first place, I need a standard of comparison by which to judge the size of the object. Thus, if my perceptive organs or sensors were located in a vacuum, without possibility of comparison with other objects, I would be unable to make that differentiation. Then, also the seeing of an outline of the object, with its obvious delimitations, equally obviously needs a standard for my organ of perception. That is, my eye sees a definite range in the spectrum of visible light. Suppose my eye were responsive to a different wave-length range than is presently the case. Then the object would be perceived quite differently, would it not? It would have an entirely different size, appearance, and therefore be a different object to the percipient than that presently perceived. And in the presence of a different medium of communication between the object and the observer, in the form of my body-mind and senses, there may well not be any observable boundaries to the "object." I would then not be able to perceive the object at all or, put in a different way, to the observer the object would not even "exist"!

At this point, it becomes quite clear that the observer and the object are one continuum and it is absurd to talk of the "object" existing in its own right, apart from the observer, as is the current conventional view. Now read "world" for "object" and once again it becomes clear that the world does not exist apart from myself. It is body, mind and senses that collectively have spawned the entire world! But by the same reasoning — or better, through inquiry — it is now seen that this newly acquired insight applies equally to body-mind and senses. Even these do not exist as entities by themselves!

Ultimately, they too dissolve into something else, into the Infinite. Continuous verbal usage through millennia of slavish conceptual adherence have lent them the appearance of pseudo-reality. Only the self-luminous I-Principle can be said to exist with certainty, which is that to which I always have immediate non-conceptual access without going through the mind and senses and to which direct reference is made by the term "I." Once again, I am That alone, and That is a birthless and deathless principle. Thus, we have proved the truth of *advaita* in yet another fashion.

Chapter Eight

Devotion and Knowledge

The two main approaches to realization — devotion (*bhakti*) and knowledge (*jnana*) — are well exemplified in modern times by Swami Ramdas and Sri Nisargadatta Maharaj, respectively. Although at first glance, these paths appear to be poles apart, upon closer examination one finds that the same vital ingredients are needed to succeed in each. They are Grace and Persistence; without Grace nothing can be done and there will not be the Persistence, which is really the energy, the driving force, behind the endeavor. Swami Ramdas, as it becomes beautifully clear from his autobiographical work *In Quest of God*, sets out for his pilgrimage through India with the attitude that no matter what "untoward" things befall him, he will accept them "grace"-fully, without any reservation, as being the work of his beloved Ram — that is, God. Since he and Ram are ultimately one, a persistent attitude of total acceptance is in order and to be acquired through continuous practice. In this *sadhana*, all obstacles that come his way are seized as learning opportunities. Here the goal is the melding of God and creature as though this is already a living reality right from the start of the search. All happenings are accepted as divinely ordained and all thoughts and fantasies about them are rejected as false ramblings of a faulty mind machine. This is not to be confused with repression, which takes place in thought and represents the forceful denial of one desire by another, leading only to conflict in the mind. Swami Ramdas' way, on the other hand, is a cheerful acceptance of events as they unfold, and through this attitude he is at every moment forcefully drawn into the Now. There is the implicit acknowledgment that notwithstanding appearances to the contrary, whatever develops is part of a superior master plan that has an ultimate goodness or — perhaps better, "Godness" — about it, which is beyond mere human evaluation. Ramdas' basic posture is well expressed in the *Ashtavakra Gita*: "The wise man is contented whatever comes to him; he wanders about at will, and rests wherever the sunset overtakes him."

Sri Nisargadatta Maharaj, the modern exemplar of the path of knowledge, starts from a different perspective yet reaches the same goal. He once clearly stated, in his work *The Ultimate Medicine*, that of all the great Hatha Yogis, he is the greatest. This is not a statement by someone with a swollen head, as might appear at first glance, since in the same breath Maharaj explains that one meaning of the term Hatha is "persistence." And he certainly has been persistent in following his guru's advice in meditating on his beingness or "I-am-ness" until its entire secret was revealed. For three years he did just that, meditating upon the meditator, until the highest state, the Absolute (*Parabrahman*) was reached and there could be no further meditation, since meditation can take place only in duality and there was no more duality for him.

Although the above-mentioned approaches to real-ization may seem almost diametrically opposed, on closer examination, this does not seem to be wholly true. In devotion there is a surrender of what one desires in deference to what fate has in store for one at any moment. I sense echoes of the Christian adage "Not my will be done, but Thine."

Why is there a desire at all? Why are certain actions preferred over others? How does that initial stirring of thought (*sankalpa*) or original intent come about? Because of an idea in the mind, the idea that one is "someone," rather than the Totality (which is only another term for "Nothingness" on the level of beingness) — the same impulse that gets one going upon waking from deep sleep. Immediately, one falls into the grip of the inherent tendencies (*vasanas*) of the mind. Thus, it may be said that in devotion the essential practice is to ignore the body-mind entity and its emotional baggage until this continued disregard leads to the actual disappearance of the false "I." It is being continually ignored and downgraded to such an extent that finally its energy is exhausted and just gives up its futile efforts. To quote again from the *Ashtavakra Gita*: "There is no time and no age in which men are free from the pairs of opposites. He who disregards them, content with whatever comes, obtains perfection."

Now in the path of knowledge, one's point of departure is quite different. The attention, which is at first quite diffuse, is concentrated increasingly on the body-mind's workings. The meditator meditates on himself only. From the gross body-mind entity one descends to the more refined underlying states of beingness or knowingness, all the while diving further into one's origin until finally arriving at the primary matrix. At this point one has stripped the empirical "I" of all pretenses which had resulted from a fundamental misunderstanding: the erroneous identification with a false center. Then nothing remains but the Consciousness, a state of pure witnessing. Thus, the approach through knowledge similarly reaches the state of pure passivity that results from the path of devotion.

Knowingly exposing each stage of being results in the emasculation and dissolution of the "I," so that finally unicity reigns. Thus, one might say that in devotion, one overrides the ego by ignoring or constantly reversing or negating its propensities; in knowledge one incapacitates it by shining the strong light of awareness on it. One gets to know the "I," and particularly its false foundations, so thoroughly that all pretense by the unreal melts away.

The illusion of uniqueness or "I-ness" having been pierced, one is at once in an entirely different dimension, the Universality of Being. Here not only the meditator and that which is being meditated upon, but also the worshipper and the worshipped are one. Then from this it follows that the very last stage of respectively devotion and knowledge must be experientially identical, a total letting go and relinquishing of the unreal, the false. One simply remains with what one has always been but never known as such: the infinite Love which maintains, activates and imbues the world process. Thus, in the merging of devotion and knowledge, one's every breath, every thought, and every act has become an adoration, a *puja*, in honor of that primary reality, which is none other than the Self or the Absolute.

Chapter Nine

The Unicity of Observer and Object

We are so easily taken in by the senses; we accept as gospel truth anything the sense organs signal us. Unfortunately, there is no such thing as gospel truth in this respect. We have lost sight of the fact that the observer and the object find themselves in a relationship; that is, both parties contribute to the ultimate result, and on the most profound level it is impossible to state where the observer ends and the object starts. No objective — that is, ultimate — truth comes out of it, only a very superficial relationship or relativistic truth. Finally, even that relationship must be transcended, because a relationship still subtly implies "entities" and therefore duality.

Take for instance two persons, one of whom is colorblind, both perceiving the same object. Each will see a different object, although they are unable to precisely compare notes. Now, who is to say which of the two object descriptions is the right one? Some may argue the non-colorblind observer (I carefully avoid the description of "normal") person has got it, because he sees a more complete picture. But then who is to say that a more complete picture is the more correct one? What is "correct" in this connection? It might be just as easily argued that the simpler picture is the correct one and that we as observers are adding unwanted complexity to it — an "impurity," as it were.

Traditionally, in science a simpler hypothesis is preferred in the explanation of unknown phenomena over an equally effective but more complex hypothesis. An observer from a different planet might see the object in colors unknown to the earthly observer. Such arguments as to which object is the "actual" one can go on ad infinitum. A little reflection on this problem will show that there is no one "correct" observation, no single object description that can be dubbed as the final truth. If this is fully seen, does it then not also become quite clear that ultimately there is no object as such, independent of the observer? And by the same token, one further finds that the observer, represented by our body image, is also a mere appearance without actual substance. Thus, only the consciousness that supports all these observations is real. The world of objects and their relationships that so strongly influence our being and functioning are merely the stuff that dreams are made of.

Chapter Ten

All That Exists is Consciousness

One of the main reasons why one so readily identifies with the body is that the latter is viewed as a discrete entity; that is, an object with well-defined limits or boundaries in space and time. The underlying assumption here is that the body is an infinitesimal entity in an infinitely large Universe or World. And it has never occurred to us that the actual state of affairs could be the very opposite: the world — or space-time — is a mere appearance, a projection by the body, mind and senses. Yet, the truth of the matter is that the world comes into being only by virtue of the body-mind; it springs from sensory activity. Thus, when I see an object, I discern a particular form, but is it possible to think of "form" apart from seeing? Does not "form" immediately presuppose an act of seeing? It is not really possible to divorce "form" from "seeing." Therefore, any form and the seeing thereof are always one process in one continuum, and not amenable to bifurcation.

In the same manner that "seeing" brings into being the concept of "form" or space, our sense of hearing gives rise to the concept of "sound," our tactile sense gives rise to the concept of materiality, and similarly for the remaining senses and their "sense objects." That is why the Buddha could say: "In the seen is only the seeing, in the heard only the hearing." So observing an "external" object, I am figuratively speaking only listening to the buzzing of my own internal sensory clockwork — a mechanism that is constantly in operation except during the deep-sleep state. Sri Nisargadatta Maharaj also emphasizes this dynamic or process aspect of consciousness when he states ". . . consciousness is tantamount to 'movement'" and "This consciousness keeps on 'humming'" (*The Ultimate Medicine*, page 14).

Accordingly, my sentience, beingness or consciousness lies prior to the world and is supreme; the world is a secondary product of consciousness and not, as the conventional wisdom has it, consciousness the product of the world. In this connection, the *Ashtavakra Gita* states so pointedly: "The Universe is merely a mode of the mind; in reality it has no existence." Thus, in the split second after awakening from deep sleep, as also in the state of samadhi when sensory activity is largely in abeyance, there is as yet no spatiotemporal orientation, but purely a sense of "beingness," of presence — not a sense of "someone" being present.

In sum, since one has falsely viewed the body as a finite entity within the world, one has identified with it as a subject, thereby creating and maintaining an unreal "I" entity and ipso facto the most fundamental schism or duality in our world view which henceforth governs our every thought and action. However, the real situation is as follows: The only true Subject is the consciousness; no "objects" as such exist, for they appear only in and as part of that consciousness. Also, because of their constantly changing nature, the objects have no inherent reality. If *advaita* has any tenet, then surely this is it. Because this consciousness is on its own and represents the Totality, it is necessarily our very Self — a Self that is immortal, because it is prior to Time, and infinite or immeasurable because it is prior to Space.

Chapter Eleven

Primordial to Space-Time

In Indian spirituality, a commonly accepted insight is that only the Unchanging can properly observe the changeful — a thesis with which many in the West have some difficulty. In fact, the idea of the Unchangeful in itself is subject to skepticism. Many years ago, when I was perhaps overly influenced by J. Krishnamurti, I became painfully aware of this schism, when I had a conversation with Swami Prabhavananda at the Vedanta Temple in Montecito. According to Krishnamurti, nothing permanent ever exists: all things are in a perpetual flux. In *Advaita Vedanta*, on the other hand, only the Unchangeful is real; all changeful things are *maya* or illusory.

At the time, I could not see the Swami's point of view. It has since then become clear to me that behind all transient things lies a permanent background, but when using the term "permanent," I don't mean a time referent, but refer to a timeless state — a state primordial to space-time. Since space-time is ever within thought, I am pointing to

That to which thought occurs, namely Consciousness or the Self.

How could one assign reality to the changeful? What exactly is it to which Reality is assigned? At any moment that particular "what" is commuted into something else, ad infinitum. Therefore, it is very clear to me that no reality can ever be assigned to the changeful. Only the Changeless is the Real, and is therefore the Ultimate Yardstick.

Chapter Twelve

"I am Not Going Away. Where Could I Go?"

Sri Ramana Maharshi, just before his death when the devotees were grieving over his imminent departure, reassured them with the above statement. What is the meaning of these immortal words?

We have the idea that upon death, we are going somewhere, we are departing from this earth, from this world. It is necessary and, I think, very fruitful to thoroughly investigate this situation for oneself. In the first place, what really is "here" and is one ever going anywhere? Also, what is "now" and what is the future? Are not these terms always a function of body-mind-sense activity? In the waking state, I can assert that I find myself "here" (or at such and such a place) in the present. I have a sense of presence, which is a direct function of my being conscious. In the absence of body-mind-sense activity, where is "here" and where is "there"? And when the senses are dormant, such as in the deep sleep state, where are "here" and "now"? It must be obvious that the sense of location and time are a direct result of somatic activity and not absolute "givens."

Now it may be objected that my sense of being here is confirmed every step of the way by my fellow beings, who can confirm that I am here with them, in the present moment. But is not every one of them, without exception, equally a product of body-mind-sense activity in their determination of what is "here and now"? Is there even one human being who possesses a sense of absolute location and time divorced from physiological-mental activity, who can serve as an independent referee or reference point to others? Obviously, there is not. Therefore, the only "certain knowledge" individuals have in the matter is based on "hearsay."

Einstein proved that an observer's location could never be determined in absolute space and time. Now we are taking this one step further and point to the truth that ultimately, that is, absolutely speaking, no space and time exist at all — not even "relativistic" or relative space-time — and therefore no "separate" beings exist. We must state emphatically that to be aware of space-time rests on an initial descent into "physicality." This phase, in turn, germinates as a sense of identity derived from identification with a certain form "presented" (that is, manufactured) by the senses, and psychologically as an impression left in the collective consciousness, an image impressed on our supposed fellow-beings — friends and family.

This image may have a certain status and give rise to various emotive states or engender pleasure. All that is involved in the resulting feeling of "being someone," which is never examined but taken as a "given." One has fallen in love with one's own form, one's own image, as it were. Practicing *vichara* (the way of inquiry) into the self, as enjoined by Sri Ramana Maharshi, especially its spatiotemporal aspects, frees one from the suffocation of the unreal relationship. If one is fearless in one's endeavor, one is bound to arrive at the liberating truth of the nonlocal nature of self or the emptiness of ego. This basic discovery culminates in the unraveling of the entire web of *Maya* and the re-establishment of one's original unicity.

Thus, when meditated upon in this way, the words of the Maharshi acquire a new meaning when he states with complete certainty that he would not go anywhere, that in the deepest sense he would always be with his devotees, in fact with anyone who would recognize Him for what he really is, their very Self, the Consciousness, which is prior to space and time.

Chapter Thirteen

Beingness is Not the Ultimate State

Once Sri Nisargardatta remarked that one day scientists would be writing about his teaching. There is some delicious irony here and also something highly instructive, because of what Maharaj himself had said about science and scientists. He particularly stressed the limitation of science when it comes to spirituality and the discovery of the Ultimate. For instance, in *The Experience of Nothingness*, he puts the position of the scientist in proper perspective when stating: "How long can the best of scientists keep his life force going? Does he have any control over it? No one has control . . . The life force has come spontaneously, and it will go spontaneously." And also: "The scientist cannot make a discovery about himself . . . What is a scientist: The scientist as such is only the essence of the food he has eaten. So how can he do any research on the nature of that essence which is he? The food essence that is the scientist, when that is dried up, where is the scientist?"

One of Maharaj's devotees once called him "the supreme doctor of life and death, whose medicine comes through his words," and one can fully agree with that. Yet, on account of Maharaj's courageous, untrammeled searching into areas where few, if any, had ventured before, I would make the case for proclaiming Maharaj also as a scientist par excellence, since his teachings are based on facts, as in the hard sciences, and not on conjecture. Therefore, he must be considered the supreme researcher who truly in the spirit of science is driven to transcend the very methods of science and so goes beyond any limitations!

In making these observations, I am particularly thinking of the way that Maharaj transcends the condition of "I"-consciousness into that of beingness, but unlike many other spiritual teachers does not stop there. Beingness is not the ultimate state, he announces; it, too, has to be transcended. Once the spell of body-identification is broken, the ego is completely exposed and, by virtue of this fact, dissolves into the manifest consciousness. Now, Maharaj says, don't stop there. Even that consciousness I am not. Recede further! Only then the ultimate Self or the *Parabrahman* is reached.

How is one to understand all that? For the state of beingness or knowingness to exist, a somatic basis must be present. For sentience to be, a physiological or physical basis is essential. Now some apparently make the assumption that a somatic basis is always available. But according to Hindu cosmology, the Universe goes through cycles of creation and destruction, spanning eons, not too dissimilar to some modern scientific theories of the birth and extinction of the physical Universe, like the so-called Big Bang Theory. Within Maharaj's perspective, the consciousness is there only so long as the five elements are present; upon their dissolution the consciousness is also finished. But the knower of the consciousness, the Absolute state, is not affected. In *The Ultimate Medicine*, he states: "Even when everything was burning in the hole, and there was total destruction, I was merely watching. Just being in a state of witnessing, I was untouched by anything." And perhaps most instructively: "So only when form is present and the consciousness is there, you feel the pain or the misery. And when there is no form, there is no consciousness, and no feeling of any pain or anything."

Maharaj's science-spirituality lesson has given us a supreme message, which is: Even the beingness has to be transcended; it must be seen that the beingness is still an incomplete state, because it is not the Eternal.

Chapter Fourteen

Hypnotized by Body-Mind

Generally, people believe that they are the body-mind, since they have accepted the concept from a very early state in their conscious existence. When one tries to persuade them that the truth is the very opposite, there are always persons who cannot accept this. They will continue to believe in an imaginary personhood and persist with this false identification, no matter what. They will firmly state "I am the body" and cannot be dissuaded from this idea. The way to deal with those persons is to provisionally accede that they are indeed the body if they wish to believe so, but then to ask this follow-up question: What exactly do you mean by "body"?

To say one is the body, one must be able to define the location and nature of that body exactly, otherwise the statement has no meaning. What and where exactly is the body? The person thus challenged will get back with the only possible answer: "My body is the form I clearly perceive through my mind and senses." To which the only logical retort is: "What is the basis for your mind and senses? Are not the senses and mind inextricably associated with and dependent upon that particular body you claim to be?" It will at once become clear that in defining and locating the body, one is "begging the question," or indulging in a circular argument, which makes the initial thesis "I am the body" meaningless. The situation is like a dog trying to catch its own tail, an impossible undertaking.

Additionally, it may be pointed out that in locating the "form" of the body, sense perceptions are always a matter of relativity. For example, visual boundaries of a perceived object are dependent upon the range of frequencies of light that the human eye is capable of detecting. The narrow band of frequencies the human eye is capable of perceiving determines the shape or outline of the body. The above considerations make the "body" indeterminate and thereby the "I" in the statement "I am the body" meaningless. The imagined boundaries are actually nonexistent — again projected by the entity in question itself — and one's body is no different than the Universe itself. Thus, on a deeper level one can then come back with the statement that Yes, you are indeed the body, but that "body" comprises all the bodies of living beings, and yes, you are the mind, but here "mind" includes the entire consciousness of all beings, the universal manifest, as Sri Nisargadatta Maharaj calls it.

Chapter Fifteen

On "Birth" and "Death"

The word "death" brings forth powerful emotions. Most of us equate the term with total extinction, which goes against the grain of our essential make-up, and elicits our survival instinct. A few see death as an escape from a difficult existence and welcome it. Some others again see death as the transition towards a new beginning. While these various fears, hopes and ideas abound, I feel that few of us have gone sufficiently deeply into the matter of what the term "death" really signifies. First of all, is death (total) extinction? When we talk about something dying, we normally mean that something becomes extinct or ceases to exist; it becomes instantly transformed into "nothingness."

Now I question this particular understanding of "death," and I think it is closely connected with the question of "birth," which is the very reverse: the transformation of nothing into something. Let us for a moment stick with the latter process and see if it is at all plausible or even possible. There is a state of "nothingness" and suddenly there is "something." For this transformation to be possible, there must be some third factor like a catalyst to effect this transformation. For it must be apparent that by the inherent nature of the given, namely "nothingness," there can be no birth, no transformation into "something-ness" without an extraneous factor. A vacuum or total emptiness can logically never give rise to anything but itself — it must forever remain a vacuum.

Now let us admit the possibility of a catalyst, that is, some third factor apart from "somethingness" and "noth-ingness," which might facilitate such birth taking place. In the first place, the presence of such a catalyst would, of course, immediately invalidate the thesis of "nothing-ness," since it would have no legitimate presence. But even allowing for that anomaly and giving the catalyst perhaps some ethereal nature, the consequence of the catalyst's presence confronts us with the following para-dox. For its presence would logically never allow the nothingness to persist for even one microsecond. It would instantly transform (all) nothingness into some-thingness! Therefore, our conclusion must inevitably be that there has never been or can ever be such a thing as nothingness giving rise to anything — in other words, there is no "birth" at all.

Now what about the reverse, namely "death"? We are dealing here with the exactly opposite situation: the transformation of "something" into "nothing." I maintain that this is equally impossible as the previously sketched situation. If this transformation were possible at all, then no thing could ever exist: it would instantly be converted into nothingness. Just as you can't get something out of nothing, so you can't get nothing out of something!

Our conclusion then is that neither birth nor death actually exists; they are mere words or concepts without reality content. Even on the logical or conceptual level it can be shown, as we have done here, that they lead to basic and inherent contradictions, invalidating our initial assumptions.

Now, one might say: "What about killing?" Isn't that reducing something to nothing? No, it is not. When we say someone got "killed," we are begging the question as to what is really meant by that term. As long as we do not understand the meaning of "death," strictly within this context, we are not allowed to use such terms as "killing" or "putting to death," because the latter represent the very Unknown that is to be clarified or vindicated in the first place. The situation is very similar to a person on the path of self-inquiry who is told he is not permitted to use the term "I," since the latter is the very thing that is under examination and needs to be finally discovered and defined. In sum, it is only too easy to be bogged down in the false logic of faulty semantics.

The crucial issue here is: Can *something* (or someone) ever be reduced to *nothing*? I say the two realms are mutually exclusive, and one of them must be imaginary or untrue (i.e., self-contradictory). Representing Existence and Nonexistence, they can have no contact with each other nor can they be converted into one another. Thus, if a thing were to become no-thing or "nothing," where would or could it go? And, perhaps, equally to the point, why and how could it ever have *come into existence* (necessarily from "nothingness") in the first place unless it had always been in existence? Even to talk of "nothing" is not really permitted, since at no time do or can we have any experience of nothingness (and it can therefore not be legitimately conceptualized). Strictly speaking, the word — which is a projection from the fully experiential "thingness" — should not even be in our dictionary!

In *The Nectar of Immortality* (p. 5), Sri Nisargadatta Maharaj clearly denies the possibility of an existential vacuum at any time when he states: "Before conception, whatever state exists, that is your most natural perfect state, *it always prevails*. When this beingness goes, that state will still be there." And similarly, Sri Atmananda states: "It is in Consciousness that objects rise. Therefore when they disappear, what remains over is this Consciousness and not nothingness."

Finally, we have already seen that birth is a non-event; then, if death were possible, we would have a one-way process on our hand, the conversion of thingness into nothingness, or "isness" into "non-isness," and soon the world would be nonexistent. But the latter statement implies that all that *is* would have emptied itself out long ago into non-isness. Thus, by saying that, we immediately restate the impossibility for nothingness to exist. Therefore, neither birth nor death is true, or possible. We must stop talking about death and dying, and accept our true state of immortality. The next step then — and it is the more portentous and difficult one — is to find out what it is that is neither born nor dies.

Regardless of superficial appearances and impressions, at no time is there an elimination or destruction of that which exists. In other words, at no time "nothing" comes into being. In a sense, therefore, one might say that ontologically the term "nothing" should be deleted from our working dictionary — which is exactly what the Greek philosopher Parmenides recommended when he stated: "You cannot know Non-Being, *nor even say it*." This conclusion may at first seem counterintuitive, yet even science points to the same truth through its mass-energy equivalence formula, $E=mc^2$, indicating that nothing ever truly disappears into "zero existence." If matter is "destroyed," it reappears as energy in the exact amount indicated by the formula, and vice versa. More generally, though the appearance of a thing — that is, its particular manifestation — may undergo various changes, yet what *is* — its underlying reality — remains ever the same.

Chapter Sixteen

What Really Is Meant by the Term "Existence"?

When using that word — and it is one of the most glibly used words in our language — we immediately, inevitably, introduce or create Time. "There is Existence," "something exists" — these terms refer to something existing or existent. That is, we stipulate some entity must have been present for at least a split second prior to the perception giving rise to our statement. If I say "The world exists," we think of something that has been there for a very long, maybe even an infinitely long, period, although "long" is purely relative and ultimately related to a human time scale, such as our life span. We definitely do not think it has come into existence at the very moment of its perception, yet if the truth be told it is exactly that! The point is that there is no world without "perceiver": it is the latter who creates the world through the very fact of being conscious. Consciousness spontaneously leads to perception, and so to the inference that a world exists, the notion of

Existence. Existence is therefore synonymous with being conscious, being awake or aware.

For example, I look at some impressive ocean and mountain scenery. The beauty of the scenery gives me an overwhelming sense of my own insignificance and the grandeur of Nature. This reinforces the impression of my being of secondary importance in the scheme of things, something almost extraneous, in a reality that hardly acknowledges me. My own being seems ephemeral and my surrounding eternal. The first part of this statement is indeed a correct intimation of my real nature, but is only true on one level of understanding. As to the second part, the apparent permanency of my surrounding, it is the over-powering impact of my perception that reinforces my basic misconceptions about "self" and what seems to lie outside of that "self." For on the deepest level, the truth is that the grandeur of Nature isn't something that exists as separate and external to my being, but that in fact my own self — my true essence — incorporates and creates that field of vision and experience. Perhaps this is where one of the greatest stumbling blocks lies to the correct under-standing of *Advaita*.

Let us for a moment look at the situation from a dif-ferent angle. Analyzing the mechanism of perception, I may state that nerve impulses originating at the retina proceed along the optic nerve to the brain where they are "decod-ed," resulting in what I see — that is, what I say that I see — ocean and mountains. For lack of a better term we used that word "decoded," but the term is begging the question, being inadequate and misleading since it assumes that there is a definite, concrete reality existing somewhere in its own right, independent of any observer, and that to reach it my sensory input — i.e., nerve impulses — must be transcribed in a certain way. This representation, however, is merely an ingrained way of thinking, based on lack of reflection, a lack of inquiry into the matter. It is also much more comfortable to believe this, since it gives our existence a foothold. Psychologically, we crave for such a solid base, as otherwise existence appears to us dangerously ephemeral and uncertain. Our acceptance of an Absolute that lies at the base of perception — what Sri Nisargadatta Maharaj calls the "objectivization" of our existence — provides an apparent sense of stability and security, constituting one of the preconditions for the arising and nurturing of an ego.

In the present inquiry, we are not at all concerned with the exact nature of the object of perception, only with the fact that I observe certain shapes, having apparent textures, and a panorama of light effects — shades of light and dark — all of which I call "ocean and mountain scenery." Upon my losing consciousness, everything would vanish, even though the eyes may be wide open. When I am asleep, there is just nothing; the whole world has disappeared. To my "self," in the aspect of its phenomenal existence, I am nonexistent, yet that self in its more fundamental aspect continues unabated; otherwise I would not be able to wake up.

Two important inferences can be made. First, it affirms our statement at the outset of this chapter that without the perceiver there is no world to be perceived; the "subject" and the "object" are not two separate entities but form one continuum, one process. As Sri Ramana Maharshi proclaimed: "Apart from the seer there is no seen." Second, within this perceptive mechanism it is really the brain, as end station, that is the ultimate perceiver, that sees, not the senses. Therefore, Existence — that is, the observable world of space-time — may be said to be simply a byproduct of brain function, just as bile is a secretion from the liver. In other words, it results from oxygenation taking place in brain cell tissue and so is essentially a neurological reaction. From this point of view, consciousness amounts to nothing more than a chemical reaction on a cell interface. This, incidentally, may be considered to be the western, scientific counterpart of Sri Nisargadatta Maharaj's explanation that the "I-am-ness," the beingness or consciousness, comes about through the interplay of the five elements and the three *gunas* (attributes) in millions of combinations and permutations — a purely mechanical process that in itself has nothing personal about it. The apparent "I" or personal element, and with it the whole *Mayaic* world of Duality, comes about subsequently through superimpositary processes entailing memory and identification. When all this is thoroughly understood, there is at once a transcendence of the ego.

There is, however, still more transcending to be done if one wishes to reach the very Existential ground of that ego. For, ultimately, that which we have called "neurological reaction" remains a mysterious event, a causeless cause. In the first place, since the brain is itself also part of the world perceived, we must drop the classifying term "neurological" and simply call it "reaction"; that is, consciousness is reaction. Basically, we are faced with a chicken-and-egg type of situation, for there never is a physical, neurological apparatus in place prior to, or outside of, that consciousness; rather, the reverse is the case.

Second, even this term, this concept, will have to be refined. For "reaction" presupposes something extant that can react, and within the present context this presupposition is impermissible, for it is existence that has to be understood and defined in the first place. Therefore, lest we engage in circular reasoning, we cannot use this as a starting point for our inquiry; logically, we can only approach it from the point of view of Nonexistence. Thus, "reaction" is rather seen to be "action, on the level of 'event'," in its purest form — a kind of magical appearance or a "spontaneous creation" out of Nothingness. As it no longer seems to conform to our parameters of linear thinking — that is, in terms of cause and effect — this event must necessarily lie outside the sphere of space-time.

Our conclusion can also be reached in other ways. For example, it can be stated that all concepts of reality are consciously or unconsciously based on the image of self as "creature" — that is, an organism having well-defined boundaries in space — rather than "creation" or the Totality, which obviously has no boundaries. This view immediately reduces our reality to the spatiotemporal level. Such an organism or entity, endowed with sentience, presupposes autonomy of action and function. We find it difficult to envisage self as other than that. Why is this so? Because not only are we identified with Form (that is, the body), but also we take the body as an ultimate reality. But again, all that there is is a certain sensation or experience which is translated as "body" by the senses-mind continuum.

The same applies to our acceptance and understanding of "matter." Both of these terms are at bottom mere linguistic conveniences. For when we do investigate the structure and texture of matter, going down to the molecular, atomic and subatomic levels, we find nothing familiar to which we can attach conventional labels that are reminiscent of our everyday-life experience. This is because all our sensory experience, and hence conceptualization, derives from the macromolecular level. Vision, hearing, touch, taste and smell impressions received and/or "constructed" by the senses are superficial experiences in all meanings of that word; they are interface reactions and so, literally, skin-deep.

On a deeper level, not only can we no longer apply the usual attributes of the gross (or surface) world in describing what *is*, but perhaps more importantly, things no longer have any clear boundaries defining them; that is, they have lost their "thingness." Transcending the superficial level, there is really nothing that we can come to grips with, nothing concrete or substantial or, more properly, "substance-ial"; all that we find is a vast emptiness, bereft of any identity. We are forced to reaffirm that truth so succinctly formulated by Hui-neng, the Sixth Patriarch of Chan Buddhism: "From the first, not a thing is." This is however not to be taken as an expression of Nihilism (a total vacuum on all levels of understanding, and also self-contradictory because logically there could be no one to assert that Nihilism!), but of the "non-thingness" or non-divisibility of all that is. This is the essential *advaitic* apperception.

Thus, apart from that spark of what we first have called "reaction," and eventually "action" or "spontaneous creation," and which is actually the beingness, or consciousness, there is absolutely nothing. Anything that is observed, that appears to have a reality of its own, is only an aspect or a reflection of an immensity that has no boundaries, is totally intangible, and so cannot be grasped by the senses or the intellect. This must be fully understood, so that its truth henceforth imbues all our thought and action, representing a true revolution in that very beingness or consciousness.

Prior to such a revelation the firm conviction existed that there is an entity, a "doer," who is constantly driven by an urge for all kinds of action deemed necessary for its physical and psychological survival and well-being. This "doer" also arbitrarily creates certain goals and is frustrated when those goals cannot be realized; and where they are realized, there is an evanescent happiness that is highly vulnerable to an eventual reversal. This brings with it a constant state of tension, of stressful effort-making, taking us ever further away from our natural, effortless state. Subsequent to the *advaitic* insight, however, there is a powerful realization that there is not and cannot be any entity or "doer": there is only a process to which we are witness — ultimately everything happens by itself. This insight into the self-created "doership" through understanding the birth of the unreal "effort-maker" lends an entirely different feeling to our life; an enormous immediate relaxation or surrender to our true Self or Nature.

Now for that last step towards ultimate transcendence: As we already implied, for the spontaneous creation of the beingness to be possible, for the world to happen, there must be something utterly fundamental underlying it, which one might say is "more truly Existence" — some matrix that itself is beyond space and time but is ever the Source of all manifestation. We may call this God, the Self, the Absolute — it does not matter what word one attaches to it, because in itself It, or That, as it sometimes is referred to, is wordless and worldless.

Chapter Seventeen

The Meaning of Paradox

The emergence of paradox or other anomalies such as infinite regression is often a powerful reminder that something is amiss in our basic assumptions or frame of reference. This applies equally to the understanding of physical science and of spiritual matters. A good example of the former is the Michelson-Morley experiment. It was carefully designed by these two scientists to measure the movement of the earth through a hypothetical, stationary ether — the so-called "ether storm" — by measuring the speed of light in two different directions. A beam of light traveling against the ether storm should have a lesser velocity than one traveling across it. When they found no such difference, they had to scrap the existing idea of an ether penetrating the entire universe, as well as determining any absolute motion of the earth through the Universe. Thus, they paved the way for

Einstein's Special Theory of Relativity.

In the biological arena, there is the paradox of the egg and the chicken. One term cannot exist without the other, so obviously no reality can be attached to either one. To solve this problem, we have to go back to the ultimate origin of the sequence, or to the beginning of time itself. And this we cannot do at all, forcing us to the conclusion that Time in itself does not exist: it is unreal, and therefore also space — the other member of the space-time concept — does not have reality. Consequently, all living forms, as defined by their material outlines, are only ghostlike appearances — having the same level of reality as what they refer to in India as "the child of a barren woman"!

Similarly, the theory of evolution presents abundant fossil records in favor of this theory, yet the actual transformation of one species into another has yet to be established and so evolution remains a theory. An alternative view is that the multifold species are extant simultaneously at any time, as observed in the present, but they are *appearances* only (*Maya*), just as in the case of the chicken and the egg. Here again it is instructive to listen to Ramana Maharshi's words: "In pure *Advaita,* can evolution, creation or manifestation have any plan?" and "Evolution must be from one state to another. When no differences are admitted, how can evolution arise?" and the overriding observation: "God created man; and man created God. They both are the originators of forms and names only. In fact, neither God nor man was created" (from *Talks with Ramana Maharshi*).

Chapter Eighteen

"Mind" on My Mind

At some point the question must be raised: Is there mind at all? And what exactly do we mean by this term, how have we arrived at the word, the concept of "mind"? Is there indeed an entity designated as such, or is it all an imaginary thing that we are toying with and verbally repeating by sheer force of habit?

Obviously, for there to be anything at all, it must be fixed in space and time — that is, amenable to a determination of *where* and *when*? The first part of this question is easy to deal with, for it is not difficult to see that "where" is obviously tied to the presence of a physical body, that is one particular body among untold billions and which I proceed to call my own, "myself," or "I." This gives rise to a particular point of observation, a special focus point which is called "me" or "I" within a three-dimensional universe, based on the anatomy of the sense organs. On a deeper level, there is not even any body, because that which perceives the body as such, as an alleged independent reality, has been called forth by that same body — a cyclic process or an example of circular reasoning. It is itself therefore really part of that body, part of that which it tries to define. This therefore invalidates any conclusion about its actual reality. We might say that to think or talk of "body" is a case of self-hypnosis or a delusional state.

The "when" is perhaps a little harder to see through, for in actuality there is no such thing as "time" and therefore no "when." There is only the Now, which is a timeless state, but through the dynamics of bodily processes — more particularly, the brain's capacity for retention and replay of engrams or recorded impressions — we have produced a derivative state called "time."

Seeing through what we actually are, this leaves us only with the Plenum or the Emptiness, depending on one's antecedents or particular point of view. Reducing all concepts to the one irreducible "What is," or "Is-ness," we are realizing the Self.

PART TWO

REFLECTIONS

Reflections

The mind itself is a mere psychological reflex mechanism. Without awareness, it is nothing and cannot function, just as a fire without fuel is not a fire. It is awareness that gives us life, intelligence; without it, we would be no more than a lump of coal.

In a striking analogy, the mind that is healthiest is just like the body: it is least noticed! When you are not aware of your body, it functions quietly, efficiently; so also your mind functions as it should when it does not throw up all kinds of psychological problems.

We ever want to get something out of life, and therefore, by implication, separate ourselves from life; for, in truth, we are that life.

"Identity" is a totally amorphous matter. Full recognition of this fact leads to the end of ignorance and the beginning of wisdom.

Self-knowing is only to be approached through knowing what one is *not*. In one sense of the word, it is not even possible to "get in touch with one's self" — that applies only to the psychosomatic part of one's being — one can only *be* one's self, which happens when the psychosomatic machinery no longer interferes and no longer deceives us by posing as a pseudo-self.

The mind does not really exist. What exists are the thoughts only. The substrate of the mind is thought, not: the mind is the substrate of thought. The thought "To whom does this happen?" is the most powerful tool in the quest. It cuts right to the root of our world of unreality. It is the most effective in dissolving sorrow — the sorrow that ensues from the postulation of the false "I."

We all have "assumed" identities!

In the state of mere external freedom, there is a certain joyful feeling in the anticipation of all the things that one is going to do with that freedom. When one is actually doing those things so eagerly anticipated, one may find them not so attractive after all. In the state of internal freedom, there is a joy purely and simply in being part of life, in being what one is — without any dependencies on external factors, whatever one's physical situation may be and whatever the "roles" one has assumed in society.

The mind's everlasting tendency to seek stability and order for itself in an insecure and disorderly world seems to me the exact counterpart of a concept in physics called "entropy" — the tendency for physical states to proceed from the more to the less complex, from instability to stability, from heterogeneity to uniformity. One might call this propensity of the mind "spiritual entropy." It reaches a maximum upon the psychological death of the organism, which constitutes its liberation.

We strive to "realize our dreams," as we say — and, in fact, mere dreams they are, relevant only on the dream level, the *Maya* level, of our existence. This striving, therefore, only strengthens the obstacles to liberation.

It may be said that we are already the Supreme; so what is the need to do anything? What is the need for self-realization?

Yes, we are the Supreme, but we do not function as we could or should: effortlessly, spontaneously, blissfully. There is ignorance, suffering, all this is part of the Supreme; but so long as we are identified with a fragmentary vision, we are — by choice — mere fragments, and so are likely to be buffeted by every storm that comes our way. Now it might be thought that if, by logical extension, one identifies with the All instead of the fragment of the self, one will automatically function correctly. This would be wrong, however, for an ideation, no matter how lofty, is still only a thought or an image and thereby subject to limitation. Only if one identifies with nothing at all — that is, the absence of any kind of identification — will there take place a merger with Nothingness and a regaining of one's natural state. And then there will also be a knowing, which is being: to be a totality within oneself, to be That.

"Getting in touch with oneself" is part of one's responsibility for good health and well-being. It means to me basically knowing the tolerance of one's psychosomatic machinery by perceiving one's limitations — physically, intellectually, and in every other way. To know when one has exceeded these limits, by feeling that something is wrong with one's being and then being able to rectify and prevent it through natural biofeedback — all this is based on the fact that, with perfect physical or mental health, one is simply not aware of one's soma or psyche.

What is the need for religion, for a so-called spiritual orientation in life, at all? If living is a natural function, like breathing, then why interfere? Why can we not continue in our naturally more or less hedonistic mode? This would be true if our minds were still functioning in their natural ways, free of complexity, flowing with life. This assumption, as we all know, is no longer valid — if it ever was. Our minds are heavily conditioned, fragmented and deep in contradiction.

True religion or spirituality is nothing other than the reversal of this whole process of chaos, conflict, to a state of simplicity, naturalness, and therefore order. Meditation is the first step — an investigation to find out whether such a reversal to a more natural condition is at all possible, and what is and what is not necessary for bringing it about.

It is a pity that the words "spiritual life" were ever invented, for they have caused so much confusion. For, in truth, there is only life — the everyday life — which is simply what *is* at every moment. And there is nothing wrong with that life, if only thought would leave it alone and not try to make it into something that it is not.

The mind must go out of business. The mind is an instrument of focusing, and only that — it always narrows down and fragments that which is whole, that which *is*. Like a lens that focuses the light falling upon it, so the mind concentrates the field of attention, focuses it, and in the process causes distortion. Whatever is touched by the mind, suffers from this distortion, which is corruption.

So one has to learn to observe without the interference of the mind, when one's vision will be kept pure, whole.

Even if the mind were to come up with some evidence that it was an absolute, independent entity, validating the existence of a separate individuality or "ego," what would such a proof be worth? Nothing! The proof would be valid only to the entity whose absolute existence is in doubt in the first place. A perfectly circular argument, indeed!

Why do we split up body and mind? Why do we think they are fundamentally different and then seek a relationship between the two? Are they not simply modes of experiencing? Like sound and vision differ, they are nevertheless both stimulations of the sense organs, subsequently "interpreted" by the brain and therefore inherently brain activity patterns. Similarly, with mind and matter, body and mind.

Language makes us refer to the same things, but that is all it does. Between individuals, these apparently common experiences may be poles apart, but we are never aware of this because it is impossible to convey these experiences to others except in terms of language ... and there the vicious circle closes again. Thus, we "language" everything without really knowing — that is, universalizing — the underlying perceptions, and so each one of us always maintains a strictly personal relationship with his or her environment.

When we say (or repeat) that the mind cannot know Reality, Truth, on what level do we understand this? Do we really see that Truth is not an idea, is not knowledge; that it is not only the fact that the mind is limited, finite, but that the whole idea of Truth as something that could possibly be known is a construct of that very mind which is limitation itself? Once we perceive that Reality cannot be known, perhaps it can then be perceived that Reality can only *be*, and Reality can only be when there is no longer a knower.

The ordinary, worldly man gets the worst of both worlds. Clinging to his separate existence, which is synonymous with sorrow, he also fears death — the psychological ending which would heal his sorrowful condition.

We should study consciousness more — its nature and its arising; all we are concerned with now is the contents of consciousness.

Beauty is in the eyes of the beholder, as they say; no, everything is in the eyes of the beholder. For the beholder is the beheld, the observer is the observed. And, similarly, the objects of desire are created by the beholder: the conditioned entity that entertains "desires."

It is true that we are the engine of God, but as long as the ignition is not turned on, it is a non-functioning engine. To ignite one's consciousness is God-realization.

When all is said and done, what can be done? Only one thing: to stop daydreaming — to be so aware of every desire and moment of fear that one wakes up into that state in which fear and desire are not any more than pinpoints in the fabric of time.

As far as the possibility of self-realization is concerned, there is really only one problem: to deflate (completely) our feeling of self-importance. Self-importance is the seed crystal around which the entire unreal world of duality accretes.

But what ground have we for self-importance? Our physical self has a totally uncertain existence: at any moment it faces an ending, which therefore also applies to the psychological self or "mind." Even the tiniest microbe competes on even terms with our physical self for survival. In reality, what we are bodily is totally insignificant. From nature's point of view, our continuity, except as a species — which is not pertinent to the individual — has an extremely low order of priority.

A meaningful life is not a purposeful life. On the contrary, in order to discover the meaningful, one has to die to all that which is merely purposeful, which includes even the intellectual search for the meaningful. A life filled exclusively with purposeful activity is a tragic mistake. And there is meaning only for the individual, for Society ever pushes the individual toward end-related endeavors, which leads to a mechanical, fragmentary existence. One has to take a stand against such pressures, which requires an understanding of the process and infinite alertness.

Meaningfulness knows no content, for content is important only so long as the split between subject and object has not been healed. Meaningfulness signifies to be carried by a powerful current of energy; or rather, one *is* that energy which is beginningless and endless, yet renews itself at every moment.

Physical Entropy + Spiritual Entropy = Asymmetry of Time. Here, "Asymmetry of Time" stands for time as a one-way arrow.

We talk about pure and impure thought, but how can there be? The so-called innocent — except as infants — may not be worldly wise, but they live in their own dream worlds. All thought being derived from experience, and so a form of conditioning, "pure" and "impure" lose their meaning. True innocence is only to be found prior to consciousness, in the state of beingness, before the stirring of thought.

From the spiritual point of view, the most unhelpful phrases in the English language are "If only," and "What if?," and the most pertinent "So what?" and "Who cares!?" — the latter, especially when uttered from the state of creative emptiness.

You can shed your burdens only when you let go of your identity.

Man, once he has created himself as a separate entity, feels insecure, frightened and lonely, due to the inherently vulnerable state of being an island of unreality. In this condition, every impression is stored in memory. Impressions are a shield against the Emptiness, which represents Death, or total destruction. So continuity becomes a psychological need and this is the root cause of anchoring oneself in a particular environment, as a particular set-up, a particular frame of reference. The frame of reference per se is, of course, meaningless, but my collective memories — the "I" — being in it and of it, have made it meaningful.

The question whether or not memory needs brain cells, is it not another example of thinking from the body-mind schism? Is it not another chicken-or-egg type of question, on the fundamental level, which cannot therefore have an answer?

There are two alternative modes of functioning for the mind. One, in which thought uses Intelligence for its own purposes and remains the predominant factor — our ordinary state of being — and the other, in which Intelligence uses thought as a tool and only where appropriate — the state of freedom.

The mind is a totally mechanical thing: so long as it operates, it excludes spirituality, the action of Intelligence. Unfortunately, we are totally unaware of this mechanicalness, this limitation, which is so clearly demonstrated by the fact that when we wish to designate mechanicalness, we call it "mindless" activity. We are pretty good at understanding and controlling mechanical devices, but here the difficulty is that this mind is us.

There is a paradox in self-knowing, isn't there? All one can ever know about oneself is what one is not. To know all one's characteristics, all one's inclinations, all one's habits, is necessarily a negative approach to Self-knowing, yet the only one possible. For only when we fully know what we are not, can the Self shine forth by its own Self-luminous radiance.

In realizing oneself as a mere conduit of experience, and not as an experiencer, lies an extraordinary ecstasy: a sense of freedom from clinging to existence — which is the transcendence of life and death. And how does one avoid becoming an "experiencer"? By not being an *accumulator* of experience. By not in any way clinging to experience, the contents of memory — except on the most impersonal, factual level. When one lets go of every experience — simply letting events happen — and by fully digesting (i.e., understanding) the significance of every experience within one's self-projected frames of reference, there is never any residue left and so one's consciousness is constantly being emptied. The mind remains unburdened and vital, fully concentrated in the present.

Real Knowledge is to know that all that binds us is mere knowledge: ideas, concepts, images, all in thought, upon which the "me" — itself only a construct of thought — has built a psychological dependency by means of attachment.

Either one examines the outer and so comes to an understanding of the inner, or one examines the inner and so comes to an understanding of the outer. The latter is the preferred way, but in either case one arrives at the insight of the essential identity of the outer and the inner.

Paradoxically, we do not come to self-knowledge, which is essentially knowing that which is non-self, because we are too much captivated by what we are not, the ego. Yet, this is the way to self-knowledge: seeing the false as the false — the *via negativa* — to travel from unreality to reality.

The well-known writer Aubrey Menen states in his *The New Mystics* that there are contradictions in the Upanishads. For one thing, he says the end of thought brings bliss. Yet, bliss is an emotion, and so lies within the sphere of thought. But Menen is wrong when he opines that bliss is in the sphere of thought. In truth, bliss — if it is truly that and not merely pleasure — is an aspect of the Self, and therefore is no mere thought. It is not of that realm at all, although this bliss may filter down into thought. One must never forget that thought is essentially mechanical, being based on memory and the reactivation thereof. On that level, thought is essentially cerebral, whereas the non-mechanical aspects of our being — love, creativity, the joy that is not mere pleasure — are derived from the heart and reflect certain aspects of the Self.

If essentially one is a mere conduit for experiences of all kinds, what happens to bring about the "experiencer"? One way in which our activities on the psychological level may be characterized is that of giving meaning to the essentially meaningless, the mere experience. This builds the personally significant and, thereby, the "personal" — that is, giving rise to the "persona" and "self-importance." In this light, we may see the significance given to, for example, anniversaries, ceremonies; the always looking back, as "nostalgia," thereby further imprinting memory of past events in the brain. All this brings into being a continuity for a series of events, images, selected experiences, that in their totality we cherish as the "me" and which becomes the central but hidden motivating force in our life.

But using the term "selected experiences," it may be asked: Is not there, intrinsically, a selector and so an a priori "me"? No, it happens through the mechanism of psychological memory itself: the pleasurable experiences, as well as the painful ones, with the most emotional impact, are retained — either consciously or unconsciously; the others drop away into oblivion.

Suppose there were some kind of clock-like mechanism in the brain, but instead of measuring time it would actually "make" time, so that man would be able to "measure" it. (It is a trick the mechanism performs by utilizing a tape recorder type of device in which cells have the capacity to play back an impression, giving rise to "memory.") A bit of a farce, wouldn't it be, if taken seriously!? But that is exactly the condition that prevails in reality. And believe it or not, we do take it seriously, so that our every move in life depends on psychological time — the idea that we must ever get "better."Thus, we are completely dominated by this fictitious tyrant in an eternal process of "becoming"!

When I begin to be aware of my real being, I see that I am not one of an infinite multiplicity, but I am the commonalty, the background, upon which the multiplicity has been falsely projected. The painful aspect of the initial realization lies in the fact that I must drop completely out of the comparative scene inherent in multiplicity, which leads to a structure of hierarchy in any human society and from which is derived most of our thinking and action. What all this implies is that I must give up my being as an "individual," which I had cherished and cultivated unthinkingly throughout a lifetime.

Advaita reigns in the "beingness" and only there; beyond that — in the Absolute — the question of *advaita* or *dvaita* becomes meaningless.

The other day I read a survey in a local newspaper in which a number of people were asked for what thing in their life they were most thankful. One lady stated she was most thankful for the mere fact of being alive, and how it was so much better than not having been born at all.

I could not help being intrigued by her answer and began to contemplate the observation on a deeper level than was probably intended or imagined by the interviewee. Does the remark have any real meaning? For, in reality, she always is her Self, eternally; she is her Self regardless of birth and also of death, for both of these apply only to the body.

Put in a different way, one could ask: Since she compares her situation with the state of not having been born at all, then who is unborn and what is the condition of not having been born?

Meditating on this, one comes to the conclusion that the question was based on the wrong premise and therefore meaningless. All is the Self, timelessly, although bodies may come and go, and one is — and can never be anything but — the Eternal Consciousness, the Absolute. The condition of "not having been born at all" is a mere mental projection, devoid of reality. There never is an alternative for her to being her Self.

Man (i.e., the mind) perceives an "inside" and an "outside" — in other words, space-time — but, in truth, both that inside and outside are emanations of his "I am" consciousness, projections by the mind so that it may objectify itself (body-mind) and other things, the totality of which comprises the world. When one realizes the source of this limited consciousness, one knows that the "inside" and "outside" are part of something else, which transcends space-time. Therefore, one stands apart from the body — both one's own and others' — and realizes that the whole world is the creation of that source-consciousness.

How could I hang on to an "individuality" and thereby maintain the fear of death, once I have clearly seen that all "I" am is a bundle of memories which of their own accord seek to gather further memories (experiences)? (That is, there is no coordinator of these memories except the memories themselves!) Memories seek out further memories, like iron filings are drawn and cling to a magnet — a purely mechanical process.

It is not only the psychological images that we hold of ourselves, but also the body images that influence our behavior. So it is that in every step of our development, the genetically determined body molds the mind, the many roles we perform as male, female, teenager, middle-aged person, etc. In this respect, we faithfully fulfill the expectations of the various society-imposed stereotypes.

The religious person's standard of reference is Being, that of the worldly person, Society.

It is interesting to note that to be free of time or dwell in the timeless state, one should paradoxically view oneself and one's actions from the perspective of a frame of reference that contains the totality of one's chronological life span. This means there is no fixation upon a particular point in time, and therefore no possibility of identification with a pseudo-entity that could be construed as a "person."

In such a context, time stands for "body," and the dispassionate overview signifies the freeing from the identification with body and the attachments produced by the clinging to certain memory images.

I feel like an outsider being let down for a sojourn upon this earth, where I do not have any vested interests and am therefore a mere observer. Having had no say in the matter of my emergence — "I" (as a body-mind entity) considers itself strictly as a temporary appearance/disappearance phenomenon — I am not rooted in space-time. This implies a certain playfulness on my part, because it is in the nature of my being and particular destiny that I cannot take anything with absolute seriousness, since I do not live with absolutes. There is nothing to lose for me nor to gain. Hence, I cannot do many things without a strong sense of adventurousness, or fun, for my ulterior motives (if one can call them that) for any action are curiosity and playfulness.

The spiritual nature of man becomes meaningful only upon the discovery of the changeless substratum of the changeful. Man in his present condition is so alienated from this timeless reality, his real nature, that he thinks the changeful is the norm. Being ensconced in a shell of the changeful, which is the passing show of life's drama, he has accepted this firmly as the Ultimate. And when someone confronts him with a different state of Consciousness, that of the Changeless, he demands proof of its existence!

But is not this a logical impossibility for the temporal, the transient, to fathom the immensity of the Changeless? For by necessity, the temporal perceiver must immediately transform all that *is* into data of a temporal kind, as otherwise it would be beyond his grasp. This also means that there is nothing this perceiver, as a temporal entity, can actively do to embrace the timeless consciousness. He can only go from the incomplete, the fragmented, to the incomplete, the fragmented, remaining ever within the sphere of the limited and never reaching the Totality.

In this connection, to make us aware of our plight, Sri Nisargadatta Maharaj keeps asking the question: Who are you and where are you proceeding to? Thus, he points to the need for self-inquiry, as most of us do not know who we are, not realizing the fact that we are on an everlasting treadmill to nowhere.

The questions of our identity and our involvement in, and attachment to, the changeful are fully interdependent. If one truly understands what and how "I am," the attachment to the changeful at once falls away, and conversely understanding how we are held in a conceptual network gives immediate insight into what one is and exposes the mythical "individuality." Then it becomes clear that the question is not whether, apart from the constantly changing, there also exists that which could be called the Changeless. For just as the snake-like appearance of a rope is correctly identified as nothing but rope, so the changeful is finally seen for what it is: unreal, appearance only, a projection onto that which can only be the Changeless.

Not only are things not what they seem to be, but whatever is observed and thought about cannot be the real. For any observation and any thinking necessarily entails a subject-object duality and can therefore only refer to fragments — never the Whole.

The real is that which lies between the subject and the object but does not recognize either.

What is this thing that considers itself the doer and ever seeks its own continuity? Once the real nature of this "I" is correctly understood and seen to be nothing more than a collection of memories (experiences) gathering further memories through seeking new experiences, then why should one cling to life? For that "clinging to life" means only maintaining such an insubstantial entity in such a meaningless pursuit.

Things and thoughts — are they ever real? Yes and no. They are real for the body-mind only, but the latter is itself a limitation on what is Real. Since beyond that — in the Absolute sense — body-mind cannot be considered real, any observation made by or through that entity is of the same quality; that is, it cannot be real, or rather the discussion of whether it is real or unreal is meaningless, being merely a play within the field of Ignorance.

Can one imagine a greater Magician than the one who has created the Supreme Illusion of *Maya*? Each living creature with the capacity of self-awareness regards the world as being external to itself rather than internal and self-created, and therefore considers itself as being within the world, within a matrix of space-time. And each human being looks upon the testimony of others as validation for his own erroneous "world" view, for he does not realize that this very same delusion obtains equally in all other "individuals" whereby each erects his own "world" around a body image.

We can now see that this chain of delusion — a veritable mass deception — could well go on forever, if it were not for a happy encounter with the *sat-guru* who teaches that truth lies in the exact opposite direction. For the benefit of our awakening, he points out that in reality there is only one Self, which is prior to space and time, and therefore indivisible and Eternal. Like the all-pervading space, which makes possible the appearance of all things and beings, this Self is the source of all and everything but remains in itself ungraspable and ineffable.

The vital energy which in the ordinary person is drained off by the emotions to be converted into some form of action or thought is in the awakened man conserved and accumulated for the final explosion of satori.

What does it mean when we designate a man as a liberated being? It means this person is liberated from fear, suffering, in other words, from torturing thoughts. Liberation, being therefore entirely a matter of understanding, can only be approached on the level of clear seeing. Any other approach, such as discipline, exercises, asceticism, etc., must be perceived as unlikely to succeed as magic.

Pure awareness is the complete, if temporary, cessation of the process of identification — that process which creates the illusion of the "I."

There are two attitudes which must be considered luxuries (and hindrances). They are the academic study of religion, and the reading of books on Zen, etc., simply to take cognizance of certain terms and descriptions of the enlightened state.

Meditation is to be differentiated from contemplation or mere musing. In contemplation or musing, one is looking at an object or considering a concept in the light of one's previous experience with objects and concepts. Contemplation is therefore always based on evoking memory of experience and thought.

In meditation, one looks at a situation with innocent eyes, that is, as though one has never before looked at the object, never considered the particular situation or concept. That is, any immediate conclusions with respect to the object of one's interest must be set aside. This is the most difficult aspect of meditation and reduces most so-called meditation to contemplation or cogitation.

A second essential feature that must be present before the activity one is engaging in can be called true meditation is that, in some ways, it must connect one to the source of the meditation, that is, to the meditator himself. True meditation has therefore been called meditating on the meditator. After all, just as in science the value of an experiment is constrained by the limitations of the observer and his equipment, so the make-up of the meditator determines the outcome of his meditation.

Happiness as commonly understood is still within the sphere of the personal; it is a stage in Becoming and, as such, merely the opposite of Suffering. Bliss is the state which results when happiness and suffering, the personal and the impersonal, have been transcended and there is pure Being.

When Zen, or any religion for that matter, becomes "a point of interest" as a subject in itself, i.e., divorced from everyday life, it provides another opportunity for the mind to "stop," to lose its fluidity, making realization impossible.

Zen is everyday life. If the quality of one's Zen improves, the quality of one's everyday life improves, and vice versa.

The spiritual life does not lie away from the everyday life. It is the everyday life, unmodified, but with an extra dimension added to it.

Meditation, the cleansing of the mind from recurring torturing thoughts, is as important to mental well being as hygiene is to physical well being.

The truth that unless one is a nonentity there can be no complete happiness must seem hard to swallow in a society that knows the term "nonentity" only in a derogatory sense.

The strange thing about mindfulness is that it comes when least expected. Sometimes when we feel in the mood to give ourselves wholeheartedly to some momentary fascination and be carried away by it — mindfulness intervenes and wakes us up from our pretty dream.

To many people, "to be religious" is tantamount to being austere, miserable, in order to be happy in the end (in this life or in the next); to the truly religious person, being religious is being happy, peaceful and joyful, here and now.

"Nature abhors a vacuum" — similarly, thought abhors a void. In order not to have to face its empty nature — Nothingness — thought invents the thinker to give itself substantiality. Yet the Void is the plenitude of things: everything in phenomenal existence has its roots in that Void.

Any relapse from awareness carries its own reaction — such is the inexorable law of nature: cause-and-effect in events bound by time (the Buddhist law of karma).

Egoism is the misapplication of the Love which is eternal to that which is not and never was.

If we could live as though every day were our last, we would soon discover the difference between "being" and "becoming."

All psychological desire is a conditioned reflex.

Love is blind, because it is not of the mind; it is often confused with passion, which makes one blind.

What is called "matter" is that part of Reality of which man becomes conscious through the senses (primarily through vision and touch). Matter in the traditional sense of the word, matter per se, does not, of course, exist (nor does the so-called "thing-in-itself" — that bogey of Immanuel Kant — exist). Hence, the division of the world into material and non-material entities is meaningless and has to be revised. This fallacious division is a direct result of our prevalent dualistic world outlook.

In considering whether being alive is Good, we must realize that what matters is not what the mind thinks about being, but only the *experience* of being. And this experience can only be had when the mind is not.

Thought, by its very nature, must always be unreal, since it is nothing if it does not divide, cut up and separate that which is neither divisible nor indivisible, neither One nor the Many, that which cannot be translated into concepts. Hence, we can only "describe" Reality in negative terms: *neti, neti* (not this, not that).

The spiritual path, in practical terms, is both less difficult and more difficult than envisaged by most aspirants. It is less difficult in the sense that one does not have to do anything elaborate towards realization, like spiritual practices, and so on; and more difficult in that just doing nothing will not be of any avail either. In fact, the latter attitude, doing nothing, will be found to be extremely difficult to carry out in practice. One might almost term it extremely hard work.

It seems to me that not only is the social world we live in one of delusion, but worse: it is a world of make-believe. The pretension must be kept up at any cost, for without this make-believe man cannot live; he would rather die than face reality. Hence, the emotional, hostile reaction when man is confronted with the truth of life, which is the truth about himself.

The spiritual life is a tender plant; it will not grow on a soil contaminated with self. Yet all our social values encourage and cultivate the self.

As long as Society is what it is, we shall have interminable problems. Society is not different from the individual, and the individual is not different from Society. The psychological structure of Society faithfully reflects the innermost thoughts of man. Those who postulate that the individual and Society are different entities have not thought out the issue properly. Also, it is comforting to perpetuate the split; it suits our psychological inertia, because in saying "Society must change," we absolve ourselves from the need to change as individuals.

Scriptures or religious writings are related to the underlying experience in the same way that the equation two plus two makes four is related to the original perception, the discovery of arithmetic.

The degree of one's spiritual "activity" is inversely proportional to the degree of one's spiritual understanding.

It is the very urge for continual new experience that deadens the capacity of undergoing any experience as it should be experienced, i.e., divorced from the past. All the time looking for the future, which to us is the projection from the past, we miss the present.

Awareness is like a lightning discharge; in one flash it exposes and destroys all the harmful accumulations of psychological memory — it neutralizes the psychic energy that has collected in the interest and the pursuit of self-aggrandizement.

Because what is important is not "living for" but "living," it does not matter what we do or don't do in our lives. The main thing is that we are alive, and stay alive by not becoming hopelessly fixated to the past.

To judge another is to judge oneself.

Thoughtlessness is to take thought, ever fleeting, ever transient, for the real, the permanent. Thoughtfulness is, with our every breath, to deny thought every scrap of reality, permanency, and so rob it of its power to rule over our life.

How strange that consciousness should identify itself with body! Body ages but consciousness is ageless, although the identification imposes a certain pattern on it.

Any act of gratification, however coarse, any deed, however foul, is ultimately the outcome of a desire for happiness. The happiness which the average person seeks, although a complete mirage, is a reflection on the level of unreality of the desire for that Happiness which lies only in the Real. To discover this, that is, to recognize the futility of his present misdirected efforts at happiness, will enable the individual to bring to a halt the sidetracking and wastage of his essential energy. By keeping this energy pure, he unites with Life itself.

The realization of one's own total unimportance brings an inexpressible Joy, in which there is silence and the beginning of a let-go.

To think that Nature has made us in such a way that to live fully and happily, one must first spend years in stuffy libraries studying various scriptures written thousands of years ago in what now are dead tongues...

To think that in order to have love in one's heart and peace of mind, one must first spend long periods performing various exercises, such as sitting cross-legged, looking at the tip one one's nose, counting one's breath, etc.

Well, one would almost think the nature of Nature is that of a very idiot!

The religious person sees the necessity for being completely will-less, not because of any inherent virtue such a state may bring, but because it is seen that will is always of the mind, which is the very negation of Reality. As long as there is a will, there is no spiritual life.

Hate, greed and lust as human qualities are not separate and different in themselves; they are only the various aspects of the same thing: a fundamental malfunctioning of consciousness.

We talk about thought sometimes being colored; but is not thought always colored? Color *is* the thought: its very birth.

Blessed is the man who can be a ruthless destroyer of his own illusions without substitution of the "ruins" by the constructs of his imagination, for he has laid the right foundation of the life of the spirit that only begins when thought ends.

The point is not, as is so often said, that one should first change oneself before one can change the world, but that by transforming oneself one *is* transforming the world; and, moreover, that anything less than total transformation, i.e., mere reform, will only hinder this psychological revolution.

The intellectualizing mind can never find life anything but senseless and hopeless, because it starts from the wrong premise. As long as consciousness is individualized, that is, considers itself as "something," it must seek to justify the existence of this entity — this, it calls the search for "meaning" in life; and by this very search, it maintains and strengthens the artificial entity.

The source of Bliss lies in every one of us; it only needs the resolving of one's problems for it to be discovered.

The spiritual aspirant watches (not: watches "against") himself falling into such thinking as "I am on the right way; this I have done, that remains to be done," or any other purposeful movement within thought which creates Time, a feeling of consolidation and progression that lends strength to the illusion of continuity which is the "I"; and it is this very watchfulness which drives him back from the futility of "gainful" thought to the purposelessness of the Void, with its Being from timeless moment to timeless moment.

In a confused world which does not know Love, the love that is talked about, which is attachment, is hedged about with sex, and sex in its turn is hedged about with romanticism, which is an irrelevant projection from the mind.

One of the ways in which we can follow, if we are sensitive enough, the fluctuations in the life of the self is by observing the degree of all-round attraction or repulsion that objects and ideas have to us. There is also the sudden feeling of unreality that some may have experienced, which is caused by a temporary loss of one's identity, and that may be the prelude to a spiritual awakening. Another way is to observe our general reaction to setbacks and insults we may incur in our life. Following the movements of the self, it feels as though we are housing a ferocious animal which most of the time behaves as though it is pretty tame, but not all the time. I have a suspicion that it is this same observation which has led some Christian mystics, indoctrinated with a highly dualistic philosophy, to believe they were possessed by the devil periodically.

There is no greater pain than the discovery that there is nothing to be got out of life, that one cannot really "add to one's enjoyment" of it. This gnawing feeling of emptiness remains with us, either consciously or unconsciously, so long as the pleasure/experience/fulfillment-demanding mechanism is in operation; and this remains functioning so long as consciousness is divided and separative. In other words, the recognition of this nothingness signifies that individual consciousness is facing the inevitability and necessity of its suicide; but so long as it is alive, there can be nothing but despair, even though the mind may cover it over with various layers of refinement.

Self-knowledge is both easier and more difficult than we imagine. There is nothing to remember, but there needs to be a never-flagging awareness from moment to moment which does not miss a thing.

The "I" can never be happy. Either there is "happiness" or there is an "I."

One's first taste of Reality is usually a grand sobering up. It is nothing "positive," but is the negative sweeping away of the cobwebs of illusions and habits of thoughts. It is usually bitter, but when properly tasted may turn into something infinitely sweet.

Why do we follow Authority? Is it not because in ourselves we feel inadequate, full of fear — and on a deeper level, is this Fear not an escape from the Void: the very quality of being of an entity that seeks to live in isolation rather than face its true nature?

In our everyday life, we take endless trouble to inquire into certain trivial matters for which we do not rush to an authority. So why then do this in the so much more important question of acquiring the right attitude to life, a sense of values not dictated by an acquisitive, cruel society? This right attitude to life cannot be dictated to one; it only comes into being through "right thinking," which requires a lot of hard work; and right thinking is possible only when we are free from every form of influence.

When we follow what has been laid down by Authority, whether that of the book or the priest, do we not always seek confirmation of our preconceived ideas, that is, our wishful thinking? And is it not much easier to accept or believe, and then be able to forget all about it, rather than inquire patiently and earnestly, and be in a state of continual ferment, which demands that there is an intense love of the problem? Is not all following, therefore, unspiritual — another escape, on a so-called higher level, from what is real?

But if this be fully realized, then "intellectual arrogance," i.e., the capacity to flout acknowledged authority, however great, is spiritual humility: the state of a mind that is no longer seeking certainty, safety, and is therefore utterly defenseless.

Blue Dove Press
Mailing List Department
4204 Sorrento Valley Blvd., Ste. K
San Diego, CA 92121

Blue Dove Press
4204 Sorrento Valley Blvd., Ste. K
San Diego, CA 92121

(858) 623-3330 • (800) 691-1008

Visit our web site at: www.bluedove.org

☐ Please send me the Blue Dove catalog.

PLEASE PRINT

Name _____

Address _____

City & State _____

Zip or Postal Code_____Country_____

(IF OUTSIDE U.S.A.)

E-mail _____

The bad seed of "authority" is sown in childhood, with the psychological domination of the parents.

Contradiction = Distinction + Identification.

Humor strikes us, gives us a short-lived feeling of relief in any situation, however tense, because it is a relief from the main dominating pattern which holds the intellect. If we can laugh at ourselves, this humor is all the more effective, implying a break in the habit of seeing everything everlastingly from the "I" point of view; as such it carries a taste of liberation. However, this humor still depends upon place and circumstance, because it is the going from one pattern to another. There is a different, very rare, kind of humor — that of a liberated being. This strikes us all the more forcefully because it is a release from every kind of pattern. Its impact produces an empty space, a timeless moment, in the mind.

Under the surface of the obviously humorous situation a deeper significance lies hidden. Sometimes this particular brand of humor is created by a man in the face of death, when all sophistication has worn thin and a mere average person, who during the whole of his life lived in Ignorance, suddenly becomes capable of looking clearly into his nature. Such a man is "saved" at the moment of his "doom." An example of what in the German language has a special term — "Galgenhumor" (humor of the gallows) — is the following: A man called Wood was condemned to death by electrocution. Facing the witnesses, he quietly jested: "You are now to observe the damaging effects of electricity on wood. Enjoy yourselves!" Some might read in this little anecdote a striking illustration of someone realizing his *nama-rupa* (man's empirical aspect of name and form).

What is required is not that we give up the world, but all the illusions about the world, our life, the Society which we have helped to build — in short, all the ideas which we have invented and to which we cling for the emotional security they provide, for making us escape from the truth about ourselves. So really nothing more is necessary for man to find peace within himself than that he surrender himself wholeheartedly to this truth — that he is mortal, vulnerable and totally nothing in the scheme of things. This demands no mere resignation, but that we live it, every moment of the day.

Life is futile, empty, for the person who seeks to get something out of it; it is full for the person who does not.

What do we mean by understanding Life, fathoming the thought processes in the mind? Does it not mean the unraveling of the complex chains of association by which everything in the living world seems to function? Seeing the present in terms of the past, and the future in terms of the present — thus making past, present and future part of the timeless process.

All our actions are only the movements of Nothingness in Nothingness.

Life as an ego is really insufferable, being incredibly barren and sordid, but thought is busy all the time in hiding this fact from me.

There lies no future in the ego — Death sees to that; why then do we go on investing everything we have into it?

The purpose of individual existence is to break down all barriers of separateness — which create the "individual-ity" — and to become one with Pure Being.

There is literally all the difference in the world between enjoying what comes one's way, and going after or towards it with the enjoyment in view. The former is ego-less "action" — the latter is the "reaction" mechanism of desire in operation, which engenders the ego.

Only through first fully realizing one's own unimportance can one discover the right importance, the true value, of all things.

It is possible to understand all the religious books, yet be nowhere at all, spiritually. Conversely, it is possible to understand none of these writings, nay, even entertain certain false beliefs and superstitions (without their having any emotional significance), and yet "have it" (children sometimes fall in this category). Such is the paradoxical nature of the spiritual life!

Peace and bliss are not just two separate states of experiencing; when there is peace, which is not merely a nominal, external, superficial state and not worthy of the term, there is bliss, because peace is bliss. Bliss, which is the inherent quality of Being, is the one invaluable Good for man to attain; more valuable than "knowing Reality," "finding God," "being loved," "finding wealth," "a healthy mind in a healthy body," or any of the other conventional social or cultural goals.

In psychoanalysis we have the analyzer and the analyzed, both being projections from thought and unreal as entities. But so long as there is this interplay of both imaginary thought complexes, which we call psychoanalysis, there is no possibility of wiping out the particular mirage manifested as "personality."

Are not the main reasons for our dread of old age, disease and death the identification with our body, our senses and our achievements? Identification with the body means psychological pain the more we pass beyond the idolized state of youthful appearance and loss of physical prowess; identification with our senses means diminished capacity for pleasure and communication, to be "part of it all"; and identification with our achievements means pain with the impending awareness that we have come to the end of our tether, that there will be no more new achievements ever — in short, that we are "finished."

Do we further realize that these pains which we suffer are the inevitable price to be paid for the various forms of psychological gratification obtained in living within and for the accepted social order?

It must be obvious that notwithstanding any amount of rationalization — and we are pretty good at that — our dread will persist so long as we continue to operate our lives within the existing frame of reference and hold on to those aforementioned identifications. Does all this not add up to a very strong argument for a basic reassessment of the values we live by?

We think a sick society can be helped, made more "spiritual," by the man who "sets an example." But this is not necessarily so for he may, in fact, encourage slavish imitation and the cultivation of Authority, adding one more pressure to conform in a certain direction — and of that we have enough. The man who does have an impact on society is he who through his personal conduct, by minding his own business without proffering advice gratuitously, makes others think and alerts them as to their own motivations.

To return to the original Emptiness must be the utmost iconoclastic and painful action open to man because it involves the destruction of all self-images; it is the final exposure of the totality of one's pretense.

Our problem is that we have a multitude of problems, on which we dissipate valuable energy, whereas we really should have only one problem on which to concentrate. And that is how a stream of neutral sense data ever brings about certain emotive states that spell conflict in the mind and unhappiness. To put this in different words: how impressions from the innocent senses are always corrupted by the brain's thought-superimposition, thereby obscuring the Emptiness which alone brings happiness.

Society generally berates those who "shy away" from responsibility; but are they not the only ones who are responsibly serious? After all, is there any obligation to assume responsibilities, which in the absence of love, quickly turn into burdens?

It is much more important to love than to be loved. And if one loves, in the true sense of the word, then whether or not one is loved is no longer even an issue. In fact, so long as it is an issue, one is incapable of loving.

Once one has got the taste of one's real self, one wishes to remain with that realization through thick and thin. Although it may elude us at times, whenever disrupting thoughts assail us, we should remind ourselves of what we really are. As soon as this dualistic feeling creeps up on us, causing fear or sorrow, we should ask ourselves: "To whom is this thought occurring, who is being threatened?" and so on, so that we may clearly see that it is not the real "I" that is in any way being restricted in its freedom, but that all this is merely a play that is being enacted within the Self, and that therefore the Self is completely invulnerable, forever peaceful and blissful as in deep sleep. During this kind of "Self-remembering," whenever warranted, we shall have the ability sooner or later to be as in deep sleep even when fully awake.

It has been said over and over again that we worry, are pained, only by thoughts about certain "unpleasant" facts impinging on our life, not by the facts themselves. Very true, as a first approximation, especially to that person who still sees things dualistically, who views Reality as being divided into, on the one hand, the world of hard facts, concrete objects; and on the other hand, the mental world with its fleeting thoughts and abstract concepts. But for the person who has overcome the dualistic illusion, and who can see the truth of a relativistic proposition and yet deny that same truth on the absolute level, the situation is much simpler. To him all things are mental reflections, being part of consciousness; consequently, all suffering is the interplay of these mental images, as in a bad dream. In fact, any thought to him is part of this great dream of existence, and serves only as a distraction from living in the Emptiness.

It is strange that so many people regard life as one long training school in which one "gathers experience." This writer, on the contrary, sees life as a training school to prepare the ground for the insight that all experience is void, serving only our desire for "satisfaction"; and that wisdom does not come through experience but with the cessation of desire for it.

We construct images about everything because the mind craves occupation, because we compare; we compare because we constantly measure ourselves: there is always a space between the observer and the observed. We never observe from that Silence which is not the opposite of noise.

Any conscious "religious" practice is not only unreal, but is immediately seized upon by the mind, which makes it into a refuge and therefore an escape. It blinds us to the necessity of understanding our day-to-day problems and activities. And if Religion does not give us an integral understanding of our daily life — which is the only life — what is its use?

A sane society is essentially a moral society, but what is conventionally called a "moral society" is not a sane society.

To understand the significance of experience it is necessary to know the great secret of life and death. And for this, we have to know death — not theoretically or speculatively, but actually, which means dying in the mind now, while still having this body. The body is never an impediment to the experience of death; on the contrary, it is a necessary accomplice to it.

When there is this understanding, we discover that

ignorance about death is the source of the experiencer; that is, there is the urge for experience so long as death is regarded as the opposite of life, and therefore incompatible with it, to be shunned. In other words, only through death can it be understood what living is, but death must be sought out and experienced while living. Then we shall know what it is to have experience, to live in this world, without the sting of frustration.

Enlightenment means to me the knowledge of, and an insight into, my Ignorance. Until there is complete liberation, the word "enlightenment" can only mean an intensified awareness of one's ignorance and the inner work that lies ahead.

The average man in bondage, when hit by misfortune, asks himself, "Why should this have happened to me?" Whereas the right question under the circumstances, asked by the man who is serious in his resolve to understand the roots of his bondage, would be, "Why should this not have happened to me?" — and when this man "meets with fortune," he asks himself, "Why should this have happened to me?" Thus both these questions could be part of an inquiry into what constitutes the entity to whom things happen. When the nature of this entity is perceived, or rather its non-nature, the happenings are transformed — they are seen to have been non-happenings. This perception in its turn could lead to a way of functioning where sorrow no longer holds sway over our life.

The man who continues to be buffeted by Fate like a leaf before the wind never asks himself any vital questions and so never has an opportunity to break his bondage.

All one's problems, miseries, and moods of depression simply stem from the persistent pursuit of wrong (that is, unreal) values, and not from the lack of understanding of a philosophy or a religious doctrine.

The more insecure we feel, the more lost, the more ill adjusted to Life we are, the more we cherish the memories of past events, and the more associative thoughts based on the past intervene in our awareness of the present.

Does one ever take stock of one's life? Does one ever examine which activities are meaningful and which are not? If one does, and begins to discover for oneself how much of one's life has no meaning at all, is a sheer waste of energy, then there will not even be any need to think of pruning one's activities. Then all the waste, all the noise, has already dropped away, and one finds oneself at once in a new way of life, infinitely more meaningful and more intense than the previous existence that had been taken so much for granted as being all there was to life.

Do not say: "This is good, that is bad..." because it is a waste of time and energy — while you do so, you will never understand what you have so readily and smugly pigeonholed.

A man who has understood the things that really matter in life never labels his observations in this manner, nor does he nurture "likes" and "dislikes."

We cling to our memories, because there is no inward richness — they are all we have got, the nearest thing to permanence that man can attain.

It is not the bare facts that disturb us, but thoughts about these facts. As long as there is agitation in the mind, there can be no true perception, no proper understanding, of anything; and so long as understanding is lacking, there will be the intrusion of thought, the manufacture of illusion — a veritable vicious circle.

Only the free mind is a happy mind. A mind desperately trying to be happy can never be free, being ever tethered to its projected goals; therefore it can never find happiness.

Sexual morality (immorality) is relatively unimportant (harmless). What is important, however — very important — is Morality. Let us sort out this one first, then the sexual morality will take care of itself.

All one's psychological problems are homemade.

We say, "Seeing is believing." To this writer, to see something truly, in its totality, means the very opposite: the freedom from every kind of belief, of speculation, and the end of dependence in any form.

Let us first find peace within ourselves before seeking peace with our environments.

If we are discouraged or encouraged in the Quest, if we say "it is too difficult" or "I make good progress" — then attainment to us is still more important than Truth; therefore, in that state, realization is impossible.

For realization to become possible, we must have put away every desire for attainment — not as a reaction against an attitude that appears no longer rewarding, but because the desire for the goal is now seen to be another movement in Ignorance, and incompatible with the dawning of Truth.

Our imaginative life is only real in the sense that a lie is real. Desire, imagination, the mind, is never Reality — it is always either past or future, for it always operates through memory, through recognition.

You want to get rid of the ego, the source of all suffering...Yet how can you get rid of it — this thing which is put together — without knowing it for what it is? Only when you can consciously put it together can you take it apart and so do away with it. The Void, Emptiness, Let-go, Desirelessness, Nirvana, Kingdom of Heaven, etc., while different on the verbal level, are in essence the same experience — viz., that of the fusion of the thinker and his thought.

We are so used to seeing things in the mirror of time, but that mirror is a distorting one. Only seeing things from the Emptiness, which is the timeless or the eternal, brings a true vision of reality.

There seems to be a question whether a personal God actually exists, that is, whether God is personal or impersonal. For example, one area where the question arises is in the mechanism of karma. But mustn't one first discover what is meant by "personal" and what is actually a "person"? I feel strongly that God-knowing can only be fruitfully approached through Self-knowing. It seems to me that one important clue lies in fathoming the famous dictum "Thou Art That," and especially the equally valid reverse equation: "That Thou Art."

When will the fear of death disappear? When we no longer have vested interests, that is, when we no longer have a stake in anything (Naturally, we are not talking here financially, but emotionally). And that can only be when everything appears as in a dream, a mere appearance, of which one is purely the witness.

Hang on only to the sense of "I-am-ness" or knowingness, or beingness, which is the manifest consciousness, and not to that of "I"-ness, which is pure imagination, because it is body-based and falsely exclusive. That should be the whole content of one's meditation. Doing that, and letting go easily and naturally of the false imagery and exclusivity of "I"-ness which one had assumed arbitrarily, as if in a stupor, one inevitably realizes Immortality. Such meditation is a true renunciation, but there is no actual loss whatever because what one has lost is only the unreal, that which one had mistakenly assumed as one's own. Man wants to leave his mark on Eternity — by his presence, by his achievements — because he does not realize he is Eternity.

It will ever be thus, regardless of the particular incorporation.

The psychological structure of society, especially Western society, is one of being in constant denial of death. All our values and attitudes strive to concretize our manifestation as durable, separate entities and thereby contradict the fact and implications of our mortality. Time has become more than an abstraction, an empirical yardstick; it has become the very lifeblood and goal of our existence. Also, one is totally unaware of the manifold indications around us that point to the transience of all things without exception.

Our escapist attitude is so engrained that it has shaped the very language we use to describe our condition. When first inquiring into one's mortality, the primary question is: "*Who* is it that dies?" As one proceeds in this inquiry, and the personal element takes on a different aspect and becomes less tangible, a different feeling arises and the question becomes: "*What* is it that dies?" Finally, with the maturation of one's understanding, one's inquiry culminates with the momentous discovery that one is both birthless and deathless.

We habitually talk about my self, my body, etc., but do we ever have a clear vision of the "me" that the "my" is referring to?

The root of all misery lies with the body, not necessarily the body per se, but our identification with that designated as such. But is there really such a thing as body at all? Most people will consider such an objection as sophistry. But how does one justify the reality of body? By saying it is observed through the sense organs, which must be good enough evidence. But that is exactly where the rub lies. The sense organs are part of the body, and there is no way that existence of the body can be proved except through the sense organs, which are themselves yet to be proved — a circular argument! Body is merely a concept, a thought, and being secondary to the self, the latter cannot therefore be identified with the body. Since space and time come into existence only as superficial phenomena on the appearance level, what we are in our essence is timeless or eternal. The inevitable conclusion from all this must be that instead of finding our identity in the body, as society would have us, we find it in the Self.

Love is when separate beings discover their identity in each other.

What we can't define we take for unreal and what we can define we take for real, whereas the truth is just the opposite: the real is not to be defined, and what is definable cannot be the real.

Many of us try our darndest to leave a mark in the world before we die. But few realize it is much harder to live without leaving any mark in this world at all. To enter and leave this world, as the powerful words of Jesus simply state: "Be a passer-by." (recorded in the *Gospel of Thomas*)

Life is good, but only because paradoxically, death is go(o)d. Were it not for the latter, life would be unbearable. But this statement can be very easily taken the wrong way — as a compensatory mechanism. Its significance lies on a much deeper level, which only the true *advaitin* will appreciate.

How do I see myself? I view myself as being with a body in the same way that a pregnant woman views herself to be with child — an essentially temporary configuration, and a burden from which to be delivered in a perfectly natural way. What is that body anyway? The body is found to be there strictly on circumstantial evidence, as it were. The senses tell me about something being present that is dubbed "body." But according to the rules of logic to discover anything new it is only through the senses that I even become aware of that which is called "body." And so what are the senses and sense organs? They obviously are also components of the body, the part of the equation that I have yet to prove. I have therefore moved from the unknown to the unknown, rather than from the known to the unknown; therefore my statement is begging the question or a circular argument. When I talk of my "body," it is just a word, a thought, from which through insight I can deliver myself, just like the pregnant woman, in a perfectly natural way! All I know for certain to exist is "I" or my Self. And since it is there independent from the transient body, I am eternal in my real Self.

The question has been asked: What is God to you? God to me is Creation. Not: God is the Creator, for if that were the case, one would have to ask further "Who" or What created the Creator? And then, who or what created that particular entity, and so forth, ad infinitum. No, God is Creation, our very Self, and nothing further can or need be said because nothing else can exist outside the Self, which is the All.

In death, as in realization, the foreground is overcome and absorbed by the background.

Only the Consciousness is a "given," everything else is imagination, born of desire.

Effort to me is to keep so firmly awake that every effort — even, and especially, any effort to remain effortless — registers in consciousness.

Contemplate the question: Is any effort necessary to simply *be* what one is (and always has been)?

The Presence (of the absence of thought, as in deep sleep) is the Self. How simple, how wondrous!

There is so much talk about "being aware," but is not that an unfortunate expression, for it actually reinforces our state of unawareness and perpetuates our misunderstanding of self. For the expression implies there be someone or some entity that *is* aware or *has* the awareness. Much more to the point and profound — as well as truly *advaitic* —

would be the term "awaring," which is proceeding time-lessly and regardless of location in a projected — that is, unreal — space-time world. "Awaring" is all there is, one's natural birthright. We cannot do anything or be anything but "awaring" — a synonym for the Self.

We all know that the shortest distance between two points is a straight line. Therefore, I firmly believe in "walking the straight and narrow path," but not in the usual manner that this saying is understood. To me it means once an action has proceeded from a clear seeing and decision to act, never to let thought interfere and warp that action's non-dual purity. It has also been described as a "doing without the doer" or "action without idea" and occurs when it is realized that on a certain level thinking is totally useless and must be eliminated or ignored. Then, such letting-go spontaneously and unfailingly leads to "right action."

The question is sometimes raised why in *Advaita* there is such emphasis on the ultimate unchanging nature of reality, when what we experience is that things are continuously in a flux. The experience of this sense of transience with which everything seems imbued is only made possible through a larger background of permanence that penetrates everything. In other words, the transience is experienced only against a backdrop of the unchanging, just as by analogy a moving object can only be ascertained as such against an unmoving background.

Another way of seeing this truth, which is that in reality nothing ever happens, is by seeing that things happen only to fragments, and that as soon as these fragments are understood to be the unreal products of our sensory mechanism, a different state — one of wholeness, utter peace and tranquility — prevails.

There are those who profess an *advaitic* outlook, yet in their every thought, statement and action manifest an essentially dualistic outlook. A case in point is the manner by which they attempt to explain the "interaction" between matter and mind or body and mind. I have been informed that this must be understood as one in which Consciousness goes into Manifestation, pervades matter (i.e., goes into matter, to "animate" the latter). I say that in such case Consciousness would not and could not be the totality, because for this to be possible there would logically have to be something apart from Consciousness to pervade. That is logical, isn't it?

One would have to imagine that Consciousness undergoes a movement which would take it into matter. But for Consciousness, being the totality, there can of course be no movement, since it is everything, everywhere, always. Only things of the order of space and time can undergo movement. The truth, of course, is exactly the other way round: it is not even correct to say that matter pervades Consciousness, but the truth is that Consciousness manifests in the form of matter to matter! Once one has transcended one's appearance as body (i.e., matter), then one reaches the absolute level and one is nothing but Consciousness! On that level, nothing ever happens and one is prior to space and time — purely the Self or Beingness.

I have heard there is a certain teacher of *advaita* who is saying that absolutely nothing can be done to reach this state. And there is nothing to do, nothing for which to make effort. Either one has got it right or one has not. One wonders why he is still bothering . . . . Even to make such a statement must then be a waste of time.

To me, the question is not one of doing or not-doing; it is solely a matter of seeing, of being so open that one can see the obvious. Then the doing will take care of itself; that is, right action will follow naturally, automatically, without cerebration. What is one watching for, in particular? That unreal construct of thought, essentially of the imagination, usually of desire or fear, that constantly causes mischief and which is the cornerstone of duality, of the unreal.

Greed and Fear, although opposites on one level, are both the same on another level. There is, respectively, *the state of wanting something* to happen and *the state of wanting something* not to happen. Therefore, you will see what both have in common, even only semantically, is a state of wanting something, or a state of "want" -- of not being completely at one with the present situation. And not being complete means not being at synch, not at peace, with what is, the Consciousness, which is one's own real being. Such lack, such disturbance, is entirely the work of the mind. But the mind is really nothing but an endless, bad dream, so all that is needed for it to stop is to wake up to its tricks, which is the real awakening, once and for all.

Do you know what it means to live on the edge — the razor-edged path, that is? It means to live in freedom, no longer under domination by thought and concept, and yet able to draw on the resources of the mind where applicable. At first glance, it seems like straddling two worlds, but in reality there is only one world — the world that encompasses everything, yet has its own internal order and in which the objective world plays a rightful part yet never dominates, merely plays its preordained function. Then one enjoys the delicious Silence of what *is* in the midst of the most horrendous noise of the world.

When one first comes into contact with It, there is living with the understanding of *Advaita*, then upon proper digestion of the teaching, one lives in the understanding of *Advaita*; finally, there is neither anyone who lives in an *Advaita* teaching, nor is there *Advaita* anymore. The state which then prevails is totally beyond description or beyond any comprehension. But then there is no longer any desire or need for such understanding, nor in fact any entity who could have such comprehension.

We start out by seeing the body as the vehicle of one's essence; subsequently, we see things in the exactly opposite way: Self is the vehicle of the body. But even that definition is not entirely satisfactory, since the term "vehicle" implies *nama-rupa*; that is, limits within space-time, and therefore anchored within Duality. Eventually, we see Self as the undefinable, unnameable, and truly unthinkable substrate. I am That.

If one were faced with the question: What is the ultimate pair of opposites that a human being needs to face as a clue to his original nature, what would it be? Is it life and death? Or perhaps past and future, good and evil? None of these would fit the bill, for there is only one correct answer to this question, and that is mind (or intellect) and Self (or Spirit). The Self is the totality, comprising the worlds of both mind and no-mind, the thinkable and the unimaginable, the intellect and the spiritual. Because the latter is all-comprising these terms do not really represent true opposites, but from the limited point of view of the individual, they are in effect opposites for they can in no way be bridged or reconciled. In other words, no effort by the intellect can have any effect in reaching the Ultimate. Yet effort is highly necessary for cutting loose from the intellect in its futile machinations. Realization of this fact is a prerequisite to any spiritual development or expression. It is the first step on the truly *advaitic* way of life.

The question is often asked: How can one speak of reality being non-dual — that is, the "you" and the "me" being one — when observation indisputably shows separate individuals expressing different thoughts and actions? The mistake lies in the fact of identification with the body — the sole reason we talk and think about different thoughts and actions emanating from different sources and conclude there must be multiple "individuals." Just as the flames in a fire are Fire only and the characters in a dream are You only, so there is Thought or Consciousness only. In the absence of identification with the soma, *who* is doing anything, *who* is thinking? All is only the Self.

An interesting observation is the following: Through our meditation, we have discovered that "body" gives rise to the mind; yet at the same time, it is apparent that the mind gives rise to and reveals the body. We cannot say which is the more fundamental. A chicken-and-egg type of paradox often encountered on the most fundamental level!

"Matter" is a question of perception, just as perception is a question of matter — like two sides of the same coin. Everything depends on how we perceive — on more than one level. The senses operate thanks to the nature of matter, in this case, physiological reflexes of certain cell tissues/organs. This, in turn, leads to the perception of an "entity" or a "me" that is separate from everything else — both physically and (in due course) psychologically, as this entity can interact with the "non-me" or the "world" as "mind." Thus, "mind," the "individual," or the "world" essentially rests on matter, at the same time that the very concept of matter rests on this "individual" — a mutually dependent conclusion.

A circular argument such as this always collapses in on itself. This then means that there is no "individual" or separate self except in our imagination. All is only what *is*, without division, the totality of what we prefer to, and are entitled to, call the "Self." And that which creates the "me" is also responsible for the world and ipso facto may be called "God." Hence, the teaching in Hinduism that formulates the essential mutual dependencies/existences of those elements — world, God and individual. (See *Maha Yoga or the Upanishadic Lore in the Light of the Teachings of Bhagavan Sri Ramana* by "Who.") The conclusion is reached that the three — namely, the world, the individual mind, and God — are one single indivisible whole, since each implies the other two.

The operation of logic has taken us to the very end of logic, without even once going against the course of logic. For logic can function only when there are divisions of some kind. Understanding the foregoing leads us inexorably to the silencing of the mind as an instrument of realization, and realization as the silence of mind.

Once one has seen conclusively that one is no longer that exclusive structure of flesh and bone that one had habitually called "I" or "me," then one is free from any idea of differentiation in and of reality. One looks into this boundless Emptiness, which is at once the Plenitude. This is *advaita* – the insight into the true nature of what is.

What are "body" and "mind"? These are mutually dependent concepts. For can mind exist without body to sustain it, and is there body without mind to conceive it? No, each exists only because of the other, so both collapse into each other – into non-existence. It further follows that any concepts based on either body or mind are equally void. Now some may argue that although body by itself and mind by itself may be unreal, the combination of both is real. But how can a combination of two unreal things ever create anything but more unreality? All that is only an exercise in unreality or futility. Thus, only the conceptless Self or Consciousness truly exists.

Body perception gives rise to a framework in space and time that drives us, motivates all our thoughts and actions. In its totality it is nothing but what we call "mind" – basically a concept, kept alive artificially through repeated false vision and self-misunderstanding.

To pierce our suffocating illusion, we should see "body" as nothing but an easy way of speaking, a thought construct. We perceive "body" as such on account of our assigning limits or boundaries to it in space and time. These boundaries have been assigned by the sense organs, but these organs are themselves part of the body whose real existence has yet to be proved. So the whole thing is an exercise in begging the question — a circular argument!

In the same way, existence and nonexistence, life and death, theism and atheism, "effort" and "non-effort," have meaning only on the mind level. All such discussion becomes meaningless or non-valid upon transcendence of this level; one then is truly Beyond Religion.

All that we really are is an "idea," everything that we think to have "existence" – i.e., independent existence – is only an idea, a creation of the mind.

Most of us like to have some "temporary immortality" – to stretch out that which we cling to – the idea that temporarily negates our ideation or "ideological" reality – that is, we constantly negate our being as mere idea. Because once I accept or confirm my existence as mere idea, where am I? I am nowhere at all, nothingness only – a "nothingness," however, that rests on the only solid basis of consciousness.

The body itself is inanimate. It is the consciousness that animates the body: otherwise it would just be a corpse, a lump of flesh. Also, it is the consciousness that identifies with a particular body and starts off the entire dualistic process of the "you" and the "me." All thought is only to keep this mistaken view alive, and this creates nothing but suffering. For there is no ultimate security for that ego, no ultimate gratification.

What is advaita other than perceiving things in an ever-wider context ... until all things have disappeared and there is only the great Silence.

You have nothing to fear but thought itself, but above all don't forget to include that "You."

"Realization." What a confusing web of concepts and assorted rigmaroles has been woven around this term! All one has to remember is the simple truth that we were born out of nothingness, and subsequently have collected an enormous amount of baggage – perhaps "garbage" would be a better term – during life's journey, all imposed by the mind in the form of mind stuff, but fundamentally one is still this original simplicity. There is nothing to acquire or to do but unload that enormous load of so-called knowledge that is really ignorance in its most potent form. The realization may then dawn upon us – if we are lucky enough or so destined – of our original emptiness or nothingness with its blessed purity and inherent bliss, even now. How simple and how beautiful!

The real Liberation is when one is no longer worried about Liberation – one more, and perhaps final, concept to be discarded. Then one can devote all one's energies to living Life, as it ought to be lived, and that Life then becomes a veritable dance.

On reincarnation and the meaning of *vasanas* and *samskaras*. This question can be understood only when treated through bi-level attention. Upon death of the physical organism the substratum of our being, i.e. body-mind, is eliminated. It dissolves and one reverts to what one has been all along – before birth and also while having this body. The pattern of our apparent individuality must dissolve, since there no longer is a physical or biological basis for it. This pattern, which is recognizable as our personal identity – psychologically and biologically – dissipates. However, what that pattern is made of is made available to Creation or the Universe.

To properly understand that, let us use an analogy from chemistry. The entire material universe is structured from little more than about one hundred chemical elements as elementary building stones. A particular compound may change its structure or disintegrate into more basic groupings or even the elements. Just so is the human consciousness essentially composed of a large but finite number of basic tendencies or *vasanas* or *samskaras*, in infinite combinations and permutations.

The important point – and this is the way I see it – is that the personality or ego in its entirety is perishable – it dies upon dissolution of the physical organism – but the *vasanas* themselves, in their power to bind and compel, persist. Just like a complicated chemical compound may disintegrate into simpler groupings of atoms, only to be made available for subsequent recombination into fresh chemical compounds, so new personalities come into existence from new aggregates of existing *vasanas*. In other words, what survives bodily dissolution is not the sum-total of qualities we may dub by such terms as "soul" or "personality" but only the most elementary psychological building blocks – the drives or compulsions underlying all creatures. It is these very drives that ensure the continuity of psychological tensions and proclivities.

When you use that word "I," what is the first thing you think of or are associating with? It is the "body." Do not say "your body" because that is the first fundamental mistake from which all others follow.

Fundamentally, all our thinking revolves around that "I" imagination or projection. Where is thought, without the latter?

Without the "body" which "I" have (better: "that has been") projected, where is the world, and where is the mind? Truly, there is only Consciousness!

The death of the mind brings a unique Silence, in which it is clearly seen that all effort, unaccompanied by flashes of true insight, is futile from a spiritual point of view. Whatever the mind attempts can change only one's *psychological* make-up (at best) and not one's degree of spiritual understanding.

All one's trouble is caused by the fact that one has originally assumed a dramatic persona, which one then is continually developing. This so-called personality is in essence only a narrowing down of all existence. For one *is* nothing less than the totality, and how can the totality affect the totality? That is logically just not possible, and it even offends our intuitive sense of what can be. Thus, one is forced to see the futility of the many stepwise approaches towards Enlightenment when based solely on effort shorn of true self-knowing.

PART THREE

PUBLIC TALKS

World Peace —
The Impossible Dream?[1]

The attainment of universal and lasting world peace must be one of mankind's noblest goals, yet at the same time, has proven to be one of the most elusive — more difficult than going to the moon or splitting the atom. The more one examines this situation, the more one sees the enormous problems involved. In fact, it appears somewhat like efforts to construct a perpetual-motion machine, which science has shown to be a theoretical impossibility. But at least conceptually, world peace has never been demonstrated to be impossible; it is more like — using another analogy from physics — attaining nuclear fusion: theoretically possible but in practice extremely difficult and perhaps even impossible to attain. At first blush, the attainment of world peace seems a relatively straightforward matter: If it were only a question of simple legislation, it means replacing "the law of force" by the "force of law."

Speaking generally, efforts to achieve universal and lasting peace have been inspired by different philosophies and methodologies, so a brief overview of the different approaches toward conflict resolution may be in order

1 Keynote address at the International Seminar on "World Peace and the Future of Humanity," held in Hiroshima, Japan, November 29 - December 1, 1990.

153

here. First of all, there is the thinking developed by military strategists who hold that peace can be achieved only by military preparedness and defensive capability. I call this approach the Maginot Line mentality. To prepare for peace, one must prepare for war. If one is armed to the teeth, others will leave us alone and peace will happily prevail. This has been the prevalent philosophy for centuries, perpetuated by vested interests of the militarists and the armaments merchants, and culminating in the nuclear arms race and "Star War" fantasies. It has brought us My-Lai — the village that had to be destroyed to save it; the "Cold War," and the prospect of M.A.D. or "Mutually Assured Destruction." Although the powers-to-be still believe in this doctrine, it had already been disproved convincingly in the `Second World War, when Germany by-passed and overran the formidable fortifications on the northeastern border of France, the so-called Maginot Line. It seems that whatever defenses can be mounted, a determined enemy, if prepared to make the necessary sacrifices, can overcome them.

Closely related to the above school of thought is the concept of arriving at an enduring peace through the fighting of just one more war — the "last war" or "the war to end all wars," which has been a popular concept in the first half of this century.

Aside from the secular way of thinking, there are the approaches inspired by religious beliefs, and these can go in diametrically opposite directions. On the one hand, religions have spawned the idea of pacifism, that war is abhorrent in whatever circumstances and that differences should be settled only through nonviolent means. Glowing examples of this philosophy in modern times have been Mahatma Gandhi and Martin Luther King. It was applied with some degree of success in India in the struggle for independence from the British, and in the United States in the fight for equal rights; and thousands opted to become "conscientious objectors" in the Second World War and the Vietnam War. The question whether such methods can bring peace under any and all circumstances has never been really tested, however. Also under this rubric fall the efforts of such colorful characters as the American who named himself "World Citizen" and endeavored to go everywhere without passport, and the Maharishi Mahesh Yogi, who claims to be able to bring peace through mass meditation along the lines of his TM or transcendental meditation system. According to Maharishi, it is largely a matter of numbers: a minimum of 7000 meditators would guarantee to do the job. I must say, however, that the mathematics of his "foolproof method" has thus far eluded me.

On the other hand, we see that religions often instigate, actively support, and justify wars. The Muslims have the concept of the Jihad or "Holy War," the Jews that of "an eye for an eye and a tooth for a tooth," and the Christians talk about a "Just War," even though it says in the Bible "Resist not evil" and "Turn the other cheek."

Those who have studied war and peace on a deeper level have correctly diagnosed the problem as being caused in part by the fact that the world is divided into so many different nationalities, and religious and ethnic power structures, each with its own vested interests. The obvious answer, they say, would be a federation of nations, in which each surrenders some of its sovereignty to a supranational entity, such as the United States of the World. This seems to me one of the more intelligent approaches toward an harmonious world, but only as a first step. For there remain tremendous difficulties in making this work satisfactorily, as one can see from the experience with the old League of Nations and the present United Nations. For one thing, the moment such a world body would be tempted into playing politics, it immediately dooms itself as an effective peace-maker. For another, the existing inequalities in the world — for example, the division between the "have" and "have-not" nations — seem practically locked in under such a system.

In this connection, we must ask ourselves some fundamental questions: Can the peoples of the world peacefully coexist so long as the most flagrant inequalities and injustices prevail? What really is one's definition of "peace"? And of "war"? Even if a kind of United States of the World were in place, would peace break out everywhere and war be conquered once and for all? Warfare, as we all know, can take many forms; it may include internal revolutions, coups d'état, guerrilla actions, and terrorism. Within one nation, there could still be religious or ethnic conflict on a major scale, as we have been seeing in Lebanon and, recently, in the Soviet Union with the fighting between the Azerbaijanis and Armenians. And, more fundamentally, is peace merely the visible absence of violence, or is it something much deeper, something that dwells in a different dimension?

If war be defined as organized killings of humans, isn't a so-called "Cold War" or any other action that harms large number of individuals "war," too? And under this wider definition, shouldn't one have to include actions that deprive food and other essential supplies from certain countries that one does not like or with which one has a political quarrel? And logically extending this same reasoning, what about the society that deprives large numbers of its own citizens the means to earn a decent livelihood, so that people are not able to secure the essentials of food, clothing and shelter, not even to mention the most basic medical care? Several of the wealthier nations have tens or even hundreds of thousands of homeless people; they are the victims of an economic system that is essentially based on selfishness, greed and violence. Killing need not be by bullets or bombs only! And what about the regular killings of civilians in the big cities of the United States, in gang warfare and so-called "drive-by" shootings? The country may be officially "at peace," yet it is unsafe to walk the city streets, just as if there were a real war going on. Can one simply outlaw such outrages? Where does one draw the dividing line between peace and war?

Even when so-called "peaceful negotiations" between nations are carried on, it is in reality a lethal chess game, with violence always lurking in the background as the ultimate enforcer. Otherwise, why have negotiations at all? Between equal partners, without antagonism, a simple discussion would do just as well. We could leave the politicians at home and send the scientists instead to all international conferences to sort out problems.

It must become apparent that the more one goes into the question of world peace on a truly fundamental level, the more one's inquiry points in the direction of man's innate violence: Violence in the individual gives rise to violence in the communities and this in turn gives rise to violence on the world scale. This is only restating from a different angle that old adage: A country gets the leaders and politicians that it deserves! Our inevitable conclusion must be that the problem of world peace must be tackled from both ends simultaneously: on the societal level and the individual level.

Which of these two approaches do I think is the more important? Philosophically and ultimately, the individual, of course, because it can be easily seen that it is there that the problem starts and there only that it can be solved adequately. Practically and provisionally, however, and because there are no guarantees in the matter and we do not know how long it will take before the consciousness is radically changed or transformed, the other approach is not to be neglected: we must at the same time vigorously continue our work for peace on the collective level.

For a number of years I have been vitally interested in such matters, and more particularly in the fundamental approach to the problem of conflict. I am convinced that there exists a crisis in consciousness, which lies at the root of all conflict, both in the individual and the world at large. It is an acute state of disequilibrium that is primordial to all problems, whether they be political, economic, sociological or personal. Because mankind as a whole is scarcely aware of this primordial crisis, all its efforts have been in dealing with symptoms rather than with the deep-rooted underlying cause. Its resolution is the only adequate answer to the human predicament, but this requires man's spiritual emancipation or a fundamental change in the state of his awareness. It is this that ultimately determines the condition of society. Since the inward condition is always reflected in, and overcomes, the outer, ultimately there cannot be outward peace without inner peace. A society composed of peaceful individuals will be automatically, effortlessly, in a peaceful condition as a totality. Any formula for peace that ignores this psychic or spiritual component will be a huge oversimplification and therefore doomed to fail.

We must begin the peace process with our immediate environment, and what can be nearer to us than our own self? We must proceed with this action because it is the ultimate righteous action. Eventually, through increasing self-knowledge, we will discover that ancient truth — first enunciated in the Upanishads thousands of years ago — that the world is not external to ourselves but is contained within the very consciousness. It has been very succinctly stated by the late J. Krishnamurti as: "You are the world." So each of us is responsible for the condition of the world. To become totally clear about this in one's mind is man's real work, his greatest challenge and the greatest contribution he can make to the peace process. However, for any chance of success in this endeavor, it should be done selflessly, in the spirit of the Bhagavad Gita — that is, as a dedication, a pure action without regard for its fruits.

It is also very important that we have no illusions about the matter — that is, no unrealistic expectations. A great journey starts with a small step. It may well be that an idealized, everlastingly peaceful world is a figment of the imagination, a projection based on wishful thinking. In this connection, the great Indian sage Sri Nisargadatta Maharaj has stated that a "perfect society," if such were possible at all, may not be viable for very long, since such a society is inherently unstable. But if the problem is approached in the right spirit as just outlined, it does not matter any longer what the outcome is, man will have acted worthy of the designation *Homo sapiens*. And whatever is done to relieve the extreme degree of violence in the world will undoubtedly alleviate the overall level of suffering of humanity, and so be ultimately worthwhile. If a "perfect world" is not achievable, perhaps because it is a self-contradictory abstraction, then at least let it be a "better world."

In summing up, it may be helpful to quote a few lines from my earlier writings, in which I did grapple with some of these very same problems:

"How is peace ever to come? Peace can come only when the true meaning of 'mine' and 'thine' has been realized. In other words, there must be a completely different concept of self, or rather there should be no concept at all, but a realization — based not on knowledge, which depends on memory, but on 'Being.' For most of us, unfortunately, the Self has merely conceptual existence; and it is this conceptual knowledge which is the culprit, which fools everyone into accepting his apparent and limited 'self' for real. Our real Self is beyond conceptualization; it can only be *realized*: then everything will become clear and from such clarity of vision the right actions will automatically follow. The self that we now know is only a relative and comparative concept; through its inherent logic, to assert oneself signifies, to a greater or lesser extent, the putting down of others, whereby dissent and conflict are perpetuated.

Peace will come as soon as the individual is peaceful, no longer fosters aggression in the world through self-justification. Then, with the end of self-justification there will arise an entirely different set of values. Primarily, it will spell the end of nationhood and all kinds of racial and religious sectarianism as emotional and political hang-ups. In the meantime, until such a transformation has become a reality, if indeed it ever will, we must do all we can to press for reforms by whatever means short of violence — both within the legal and political channels and without — because time is running out; the house is on fire.

Universal Brotherhood and Beyond — A Spiritual Perspective[1]

The subject of this address is "Universal Brotherhood," a concept that most of us can readily endorse yet find difficult to embrace in everyday living. One explanation for this is that there is an unbridgeable gap between the ideal or the concept on the one hand, and on the other hand, the actuality of the world as it is. And, second, it seems to me that the goal of universal brotherhood, worthy though it may be, does not go nearly far enough if the establishment of a peaceful and orderly world is our aim. After all, even brothers will fight and perhaps slay each other; the Bible relates such an event. Let us also remember how many unpeaceful events have taken place in the name of universal brotherhood and other such noble ideals.

So it appears that we must go well beyond "brotherhood," if peace and happiness are our goal. Hence, the title of this paper reads "Universal Brotherhood and Beyond" and it is the "beyond" that I wish to stress and explore — how to proceed "beyond," not only beyond brotherhood but beyond all concepts, because concepts are never the

1 Keynote address given to the *7th International Conference of the New Paradigms* *"Holistic Vision for the 21st Century,"* November 17-21, 1999, Guadalajara, Mexico.

actuality. And with this transcendence of all conceptualization, one enters inevitably and naturally into the spiritual domain; hence, the addition of the designation "a spiritual perspective" to the title of this paper.

Only through the transcendence of the intellect can there be a profound change, if not in the collective, then at least in the individual. And at this point, in the initial phase of self-inquiry, I would like to stress the "individual." For, after all, what lies nearer at hand than oneself? So that is where one should begin. Later, as one goes into it more deeply, one will see that there exists a subtle connection between the individual and the collective and that any fundamental change in the individual has repercussions in the collective, and vice versa. Later still, one realizes that what exists is only a universal life principle that manifests in and through a multitude of creatures, and that the individual and the collective are in reality one and the same. In the final stage, one understands that the multitude of life forms are really some sort of dream entities and that what exists alone is the Consciousness or the Self. There any trace of individuality ceases to exist. Just as all the multifarious pieces of gold jewelry are essentially only gold, so the multitude of individualities are only Consciousness.

That state and the path toward it have been denoted by the term *advaita*, which literally means "not-two." Actually, this is a simple code word for something immense, that comprises not only a completely different outlook on life but also a revolutionary way of living and functioning. *Advaita* entails a jump into the Unknown, into what lies beyond a mind that can only function by relating fragments and is itself a fragment. In one of my books, I have defined *advaita* as "the end of mathematics," because it transcends all numbers, all fractions; or one might say it is the state prior to all numbers and divisions. It is not to be confused, as it often is, with the philosophical school of "monism." People on occasion have asked how I can advocate non-dualism when diversity and variability are only too apparent in nature and the cosmos. They are confusing *advaita* with monism. It is the latter that stands in opposition to all diversity. Its purpose is to satisfy the intellectual craving for fitting all phenomena into a rigid conceptual system and not to find out the ultimate truth. I have also referred to the reality of *advaita* as the background to all backgrounds, beyond the body, mind and senses, and as That which is its own cause, Self-luminous. It is experienced as undiluted Bliss and Freedom. Sri Krishna Menon or Sri Atmananda of Trivandrum described *advaita* as "the negation of both dualism and monism and stands beyond both. It is what remains after rejecting all that stands as 'this' or 'that'."

Thus, one could say it is an extraordinary state of Oneness or Holism in which there are divisions but no divisiveness, demarcations but no opposites in conflict with each other. Whereas monism is intellectual, *advaita* is purely experiential. I will come back to this shortly, but in the end, what matters most is not the description but the realization which lies beyond words and concepts.

We live and breathe dualism, function entirely within pairs of opposites, and so *advaita* seems at first glance totally alien. Yet when its truth is realized, one experiences the world in an almost opposite manner: duality seems unnatural and even somewhat offensive to one's sensibilities, and *advaita* feels like our natural habitat and way of functioning. There are faint echoes of what we have been eternally and cannot be anything else timelessly.

Why are we at present totally engulfed in dualism? It may be worthwhile to go into this since there may well lie a clue to reaching its opposite state. When we look at the world, we perceive a multitude of "objects," both inanimate and animate, among which is our own body. The seeing we do is always from a fixed point, both physically, with the observer at any one time being at a fixed point in space and time, and psychologically with the observation always being made from a fixed background and a fixed point of view — that is, based on certain concepts and conditioning. Thus, both physically and psychologically, the seeing is from something that can best be described as an object. And such seeing from an object can sense and comprehend the world only in like terms — as objects, too.

Now it follows from this that the one who understands and knows all this, in its totality, the Knower, cannot be an object. It is only the greater that can fully understand the smaller; the ineffable and subtle that can fully understand the grosser. So the Knower not being an object, must be the Totality, and therefore he stands outside the usual subject-object relationship, which is the essence of dualism. Furthermore, the Knower, which is oneself, being all-embracing, cannot be known within such a linear relationship. Therefore, Knowing can be said to be identical to "Being" and it must be clear that, in *advaita,* there is no question of acquiring some mysterious new knowledge, but simply of abandoning the old and false outlook. Then if one lets go of the ignorance in one's outlook, the truth will shine by its own light without the conventional, limited knower even entering the picture.

There is a further lesson to be learned from considering what really are "objects" and what is "light," and their peculiar mutual relationship. An object is actually never seen directly but only through the medium of the light that it obscures or reflects, which then falls on our retinas. Thus, when we say that an object is perceived, the statement is, strictly speaking, incorrect since we have only perceived the light. And the counterpart to this is that light itself is never perceived directly, only indirectly when reflected by an object. Or it is inferred when it is obscured by an object.

Similarly, the Consciousness which is the Self cannot be directly perceived as such; it is known only when it is reflected by an object in the mind. Thus, in deep sleep one does not perceive the Consciousness. But in the waking state, when through attention it is directed at a certain object, it is perceived indirectly. And analogously to what applies to light, it is not the object that one sees but only the Consciousness. Ultimately, one never sees an object, only light or Consciousness, and without the light of Consciousness, no object would enter our awareness. Thus, the outer light illuminating objects and the inner light of Consciousness are both imperceptible to the senses and mind, but the outer light is affirmed by the manifestation of objects, and the inner light of Consciousness by the fact that objects become manifest or known in its presence. However, in our present state of mind we are likely to be so fascinated or hypnotized by the object that we miss the most obvious and essential part, the Consciousness.

Sri Atmananda summed it up as follows: "Whenever you proceed to examine an object, take it to be an object first, and yourself the subject. An object can be an object of Consciousness alone. Therefore, when you take it as an object, Consciousness automatically comes in, the object loses its objectivity, and it shows you your real nature, Consciousness. This explains the whole world of objects and it is no longer necessary to examine another object."

However, until one has turned inward and become cognizant of this obvious state of affairs, one is likely to remain enthralled or hypnotized by the object, thereby missing the Consciousness altogether. Yet all objects point only to the Consciousness, and Consciousness is all that truly exists.

There is the story of the tenth man that illustrates the situation rather well. Ten men forded a stream and, on reaching the other shore, wanted to make sure they all had safely arrived. One of them started to count and, while doing so, inadvertently left himself out. His count went only as far as nine, so he cried out, "We have lost one, who could it be?" Then another man, doubting the first one's counting ability, began to recount but alas, he came to the same result. All the others started the count and all went only to nine, and so found one missing. They asked themselves "Who is the missing one?" Notwithstanding all the efforts to identify the missing man, they failed in doing so. "Whoever he is that drowned," one sentimental man said, "we have lost him." Saying this, he burst into tears and the other nine fools followed suit.

A sympathetic bystander who saw them all weeping on the river bank asked what was going on. When told, he made a shrewd guess as to what had happened. He then said to them: "Let each of you count for himself, but one after the other — one, two, three and so on — while I give each of you a blow, so that all of you can be sure to have been included and counted only once. In this way, we shall certainly find the missing man." On hearing this, they rejoiced at the prospect of finding their "lost" comrade and went ahead as planned.

While the counter gave a blow to each of the ten in turn, the one receiving the blow counted himself aloud. "Ten" said the last man on receiving the last blow. Absolutely flabbergasted, they looked at one another, saying "We are ten," with one voice and thanked the outsider for having removed their anguish.

So we learn from this little parable that the tenth man was never actually lost. The cause of their pain and sadness was only their own ignorance, which consisted in overlooking the obvious. This applies to most of us. The cause of our suffering is not imposed from the outside but is of our own doing, namely, a basic ignorance of what we are in our real nature. For me, there lies another message in the parable, namely, that we are inclined to repeat uncritically what we hear from others which may be quite erroneous, such as the idea that we are not the Consciousness but only a body.

Let us take stock here. Through my emphasis on *advaita* or Vedanta, by now you may have realized that I favor particularly a spiritual approach to the human predicament, not a political, sociological, economic, psychological, psychoanalytical or any of the other intellectual approaches, which in essence are all fractional. It is not just a matter of individual preference, but that which I am convinced is the only thing that will work. What do I mean by "spiritual"? Currently, the term "spiritual" is one of the most abused words in our language and therefore needs some clarification. I consider a spiritual approach an integral or total approach.

Normally, we study the world and ignore the observer of the world as though he had nothing to do with it. That is, the observer and the world remain in separate compartments, which is the essence of dualism. In the spiritual approach that I favor, such as the discipline of *advaita*, the observer is studied equally and found to belong to one continuum with the observed. This approach is therefore purely non-dualistic and although this term is normally associated with religion or philosophy, it is actually the field of inquiry into the nature of man and the world that is the most in tune with the true scientific spirit. By the latter, I mean a path of inquiry free from prejudice and wishful thinking, free also from the purely personal that so often corrupts man's endeavors.

Unlike what popular opinion takes it to be, spirituality is supremely scientific, not in methodology, but in spirit, in its purity, in its efforts to find the truth for truth's sake only. But whereas science is the study of the objective world — the field of body, mind and senses — and is applicable only in the waking state, spirituality transcends the objective world and is applicable in an integral way to all the three states of waking, dreaming and sleeping. It is surely unrealistic and unprofitable to study only one-third of man's existence and ignore the other two-thirds. Furthermore, whereas science is concerned with knowledge, spirituality is concerned with Being. Whereas science is dualistic, since it builds upon the separate and independent existences of subject and object, created only by and in concept, spirituality is non-dualistic but forms the background, matrix and ultimate source of manifest duality. And last, whereas science is concerned with the changeable and with effecting further changes in that realm, spirituality is concerned with that which never changes, our fundamental self-nature.

Finally, let us put the entire issue of Universal Brotherhood in the correct perspective. The point I wish to make is that spirituality is concerned with what *is*, in the here and now, and with living with what *is*. Over the centuries great avatars have come and gone, and apparently have not been able to make the slightest dent in the existing order. Whatever improvements have been made in man's lot have been slight or almost imperceptible. Even to talk about improvement in an age of holocaust, genocide and nuclear and biological war capabilities seems almost ironical. There has been no fundamental amelioration in man's proverbial inhumanity to man. Suffering is part of man's inherent condition, that is, as he functions at present.

Now in *advaita* one inquires into the suffering, primarily whether it is real or illusory. If one inquires earnestly from beyond the body, mind and senses, the suffering appears to be part of the great dream which almost all of mankind is dreaming. It is found that the entire drama of existence is played out in the unreal, in that dream, and there is absolutely no individuality and therefore no entity who experiences suffering. One does not come to this conviction through believing or even thinking, but only through what is called *vichara*, inquiry. In this process, a teacher or guru can make a great deal of difference, can smooth the path of the student. But thought leads us astray because it is invariably based upon concepts that are woven together from the strands of the old world view with its erroneous vision.

Even after one has realized the truth, there are times that thinking again takes over and the *samskaras* (innate tendencies of the mind, based on its earlier formation) reassert themselves. Then there is no other way but to revisualize the truth to oneself. This revisualization is particularly effective if one's initial glimpse of the truth had been in the presence of the guru. One witnesses the *samskaras* as mere objects from the point of view of Consciousness, and so emasculates the *samskaras* time and again until they are completely neutralized and cease interfering with one's stay in Reality. One could also say that one constantly wakes up to the real world from the dream of *maya*. Thus, *advaita* is really a wake-up call, and nothing more.

In my view, spirituality as discussed here, and more particularly *advaita*, is an integral effort to human salvation that has proven to be a real blessing. Needing no particular preparation or disposition, it is open to all humanity, regardless of intellectual capabilities. Yet, in the modern world relatively very few people have taken to it. In an era of increasing specialization, we are not used to an integral approach any longer; and possibly through the advent of the computer, our thought processes have become increasingly linear. Perhaps thousands of years ago, at the time of the Buddha and the Upanishads, before our present era of specialization, such a total or spiritual approach came more naturally. In addition, through acculturation, we have become less and less tribalized and more and more entrenched in a false sense of individuality. Because of these various factors, it has become increasingly difficult for the majority of people to let go of all that. For many who succeeded, it has been a wrenching process from the start.

A common misunderstanding, especially among beginning students of spirituality is that the spiritual and the worldly aspects of man stand in opposition and in some way are competing with each other. It is not like that at all. The worldly aspect of man does not subsume the spiritual element, but the spiritual element subsumes the worldly aspect and all other aspects. My point is that before one can come to any action in the world that can really make a difference, one must first have a correct understanding of man — not just knowledge on the scientific level, the psychological level, etc. Although the latter is useful within a certain context, when it comes to fundamental change, such approaches cannot be effective because they are based on a partial and therefore incomplete understanding of what man really is. This incompleteness is called "Ignorance" or *Avidya* in spiritual parlance, because it is based on an erroneous understanding of what man is in his essential nature.

In summary, and recapitulating our previous discussion: The exploration of one's being on the spiritual or total level is always much more difficult than the specialized, fragmentary approach. This is because the latter is a continuation of our usual thought processes and activities where one stays on the surface; it is largely an activity by the mind and the senses, in which the mind is taken for granted. In other words, what has happened is that we have explored extensively the world as objects, in which the perceiver is also viewed as an object. But who is the subject or the perceiver we don't know, we have overlooked, as in the story of the tenth man. And just as when the tenth man was found to have been there all along and every trace of sadness vanished at that moment, when we study the perceiver and find he is the all-inclusive Reality, free from impurities, one's own perfection is realized.

Thus, *advaita* is never to be used as a means to an end; it is not concerned with improving the world. Why should it? The world is unreal, which does not mean it does not exist, but it is entirely mental. It exists only within the "you" and not apart from it. Thus, things do not happen *to* you, but they happen *within* you. Sri Ramana Maharshi said it slightly differently but very beautifully: "The world is only spiritual. Since you are identifying yourself with the physical body you speak of this world as being physical and the other world as spiritual. Whereas that which *is*, is only spiritual."

Another way to put this is the well-known spiritual truth that what one thinks of sufficiently, one becomes eventually. Thus, constantly thinking that one is in the world and that that world is material means that one becomes restricted to the physical body; one becomes that body, and therefore one's lot is tied up with that transient entity. And so one is doomed to suffering. Then, at the other extreme, there are those who say that if we should stop thinking altogether, we may realize ourselves by becoming the state of Nothingness; that is, if you constantly think of nothing, you become Nothing. These people have made the thought-free state their Utopia. But you can't *become* Nothing, you can only *be* Nothing. More correctly, you *already are* Nothing, but because you think you are all these wonderful things, you have not yet discovered the state of Nothingness that one is in reality.

There is nothing wrong with thinking per se. Of all the animals, Nature has endowed *Homo sapiens* the most richly with this faculty, although looking at individual behavior you may not always think so. So why deny or suppress our birthright?

Thinking activity, to a large extent, comprises the necessary organizing and cleaning out of the brain's outdated and erroneous files. Already much of that activity goes on while dreaming, yet more is required. What needs to be cleaned out primarily, however, is that thought which is wrongly structured around an imaginary identity and which has fundamental errors in it, being based on faulty assumptions, the most fundamental of which are a false self-image and mistaken world view.

If through the purifying insights of non-dualism we are taking our final stance in the spirit, whatever work remains to be done can only be to constantly exercise our sense of discrimination, the seeing from moment to moment of the false as the false and the truth through the false. In this way, *advaita* becomes its own fulfillment, its own glory, and a real blessing to all of creation.

Another Look at Nonviolence[1]

I find there is an important question as to what exactly is meant by the term "nonviolence." We readily assume we know what nonviolence is. Violence we know only too well, and by projecting its opposite, we think we know nonviolence. But here, I think, is where we make a fundamental mistake, because we assume that violence and nonviolence form a pair of opposites. Now my point is that "nonviolence," so-called, as the opposite of violence is still violence, but dressed up in sheep's clothes. And the real nonviolence is not the opposite of any known state of mind, but comes about only through transcendence of the entire contents of consciousness. So long as the mind functions as a center of psychological activity, our actions will spring from violence, since such a mind itself is the product of violence, has come about through a violent act, as we shall examine later.

J. Krishnamurti stated it this way: "Man is violent and the ideal of nonviolence is only an immature approach to violence. What is important is to face the violence, understand it and go beyond it, and not invent an escape, an ideal

1 Keynote address delivered at the *International Colloquium on the Problem of Violence*, August 6-8, 1992, Gandhi Ashram, Canti Dasa, Bali, Indonesia.

called 'nonviolence' which has no reality whatsoever."[2] And on another occasion, he said: "nonviolence is unreal to a man who is violent. The understanding of that violence is urgent, immediate, and the action of a mind that is pursuing nonviolence and yet is violent, is merely sowing violence all the time."[3]

One source of confusion is that we usually define violence in the narrow sense of physical interference with the outside world. Here I wish to make the point that violence is to be defined in a much broader sense, since an action need not be restricted to the physical or be directed outwardly to be violent. A mental action can be equally as violent as a physical action, and sometimes even more so. It is well known that mental cruelty can be more damaging in its effects than physical cruelty. The violence can be very subtle. For example, how does one look upon Gandhi's tactic of fasting in dealing with his British oppressors? Certainly, it was effective at the particular time and place, even though such an approach may not be universally valid. But, there is no doubt in my mind that fasting to death or near-death is an act of physical violence perpetrated upon one's own body, as surely as suicide is such an act. Second, is not the whole process of achieving one's demands through the fast, the threat of self-immolation, or other means, an act of violence towards others? Is it not really a more or less subtle form of blackmail?

Now the reverse also applies: not every physical act, even the extreme action of killing, need flow from violence. As an example, I would like to adduce the sword fights between samurai as related in Zen and discussed in some detail by the late Dr. D.T. Suzuki. Here the goal is not primarily the killing of one's opponent, but the attainment

2 Talks by Krishnamurti in India, 1966, p. 90 (Publ. Krishnamurti Writings, Inc.).
3 Ibid., p. 90

of the transcendental state of egolessness, in which all fear for the survival of the body-mind entity has ceased.

In the Bhagavad Gita, Lord Krishna teaches Arjuna, the warrior, the principle of action without thought for its fruits. In the ensuing battle, Arjuna surrenders his will, his ego, to the needs of the moment; he has become purely the totality, and whatever actions flow from him can therefore no longer be considered violent. In either case, the outward action is an outflow of an inner condition. Sri Atmananda of Trivandrum comments that Krishna's advice does not advocate raw violence, but that he was advocating only activity or action. Whether the action is violent depends on the underlying motive, which is an expression of the ego. But Krishna had already emasculated his ego by removing all desire for the fruits of his action.

Because we mistakenly consider "form" as ultimately real, when this form perishes we automatically impute violence as the causative factor. Yet the godly principle that rules the world of manifestation does not abide by permanence of any forms; on the contrary, transience is its very hallmark. Look for example at the process of fertilization, how many sperm are produced and perish for just a few to hit their target. Therefore, that principle can never be accused of violence — maybe wastefulness, but never violence. And why should that principle be concerned about not being wasteful? Only finite beings need worry about that, not the Infinite, the Source of everything, which can create and uncreate at will.

Having clearly recognized where violence reigns, where does one start in eradicating violence within the sphere of one's capacity? Sri Atmananda gives us a powerful clue by stating that we should deal purely with the feelings and leave the personality out of it. Thus, we should hate the hatred in another, but we should not hate the other. And logically, one should begin by hating the hatred in oneself, for when that is done one ceases to hate anybody.

Again, we are brought back to ourselves: How does one eradicate the hatred, the violence, within oneself? The different religions purport to teach us to love others, but only *Advaita Vedanta* — which is the essential core of all religions — teaches one to become that pure state beyond the level of the mind, which is love itself. For this, it is essential to trace the primordial act of violence that is the seed from which all further violence springs.

Speaking strictly for myself, my initial frame of reference is that everything is part of a Oneness, pure Beingness, which is all that exists and in which a natural harmony reigns — a position I have arrived at intuitively rather than analytically. I do not think such a vision of non-duality can be demonstrated to others or proved through the intellect, since the very means of such proof are themselves at issue. Rather, the problem will have to be approached from the other end, to find out if the arguments of the dualists can be substantiated and whether the divisions seen by them are real or imaginary.

In my vision, all divisions and fractions have no primary reality and appear only subsequently as a superimposition on the unified field of what *is* by mind activity. The entire superimposition happens in and through the mind or intellect. For without thought, where is "this" and "that"? And where is the past and where is the future? There is only the Now, the immediate, the "suchness" of Manifestation, the totality — and all That is my Self. It does not matter what noun is used to refer to that which is basically unnameable, for the name is part of thought and therefore totally inadequate and inherently divisive. Thought can only operate by cutting up the Whole into pieces which it can manage to designate and manipulate.

Thus, our basic fall into duality has occurred with thought cutting up both space and time, where it concerns the body-mind process, and then identifying with the resulting fractions.

First, there is the space occupied by an apparent "body," which occurs when we refer to this body manifestation as "I" or "me." It is all right to refer to oneself as "I" or "me" if one stays with infinity and thereby remains all-inclusive. But the reality is that we are all-exclusive; all that falls outside our skin is considered to be non-I or alien, and therefore a threat to that particular atom of space in which alone one is interested and which one wishes to protect with all one's capacity. Those who embrace this false outlook say: But look, there is the body and it is quite distinctly delineated against a background of otherness. Breathing and living through that body, as I do, that must obviously be my ultimate reality, and so my wary attitude vis-à-vis the otherness or the non-"me" is based on self-preservation and hardly needs defending. Now we are not denying that the body needs protecting, but by the same logic, so do all other bodies. And while it is fine to talk about self-preservation, this already implies that one knows what that self is. I am saying that the basic error springs from looking upon the so-called body as ultimately real and therefore assigning absolute boundaries that separate it from the rest of existence. For if I cannot prove that my skin really contains my being, if there are no well-defined boundaries around the "me," then I don't really exist as an "I" or a "person."

At this point, there are only two possibilities. The first is that my Beingness is reduced to zero, and that existence has been turned into nonexistence, which is obviously untrue, for in that case I would not be "sentient" and this whole discussion could not have come about in the first place. The second alternative is that I am no longer a creature, but creation itself: I am the entire physical and mental universe, and the saying "You are the world" appears to be true not just in a metaphorical but in a literal sense.

Essentially, the argument of the dualists, that each of us is a discrete entity, is based on physical evidence. Everyone sees his body as an independent entity sharply delineated within the space-time framework. There is, however, one fatal weakness to this argument: The evidence is supplied not by the subject, the knower or the self, but by the senses — that is, the body itself — the very object whose independent existence is in dispute. So the dualists' argument is begging the question. It is like someone being considered a great person, on the sole evidence of his maintaining: "I am a great person." The fact is only that the body itself provides the evidence that it is sharply defined in space, and thereby establishes a cyclic argument, or a self-affirming definition which therefore cannot give it existential validity.

Now let us look at the "me"'s identification with time or duration. Just as spatial identification determined my physical separateness, so the temporal identification determines my psychological and temporal discreteness or separateness. I came to this limitation in time initially by accepting a beginning and end for my "self," as determined by the "birth" and "death" points. Now it is important to understand that these alleged (absolute) transition points are not experiential but purely conceptual: I only know about birth and death from hearsay. To have realized my birth, I should be able to testify to my emergence from Nothingness at so-called birth and the reverse at so-called death. But who can testify as to the beginning of his own existence? The fact is that no human being has had the consciousness of such a beginning nor that of a termination.

Now how do I really function, operationally? Any

action on my part — that is, on the part of a person or individual — is determined entirely by my present mental state. Psychologically, I am obviously the sum total of my experience, my knowledge, but this applies only to the waking state. When dreamlessly asleep, there is not that identification with time or memory because the knowledge is not available, and so there is no sense of a separate self.

In the waking state, and also in the dream state, I have a history which defines me as a person. Each person really represents a particular story, the account of his life experiences — what we call his "background." Hence, history on the personal level is literally "his-story." But even this very term is compromised, as it begs the question. For who is referred to in "his," whose story is it anyway? Whom do these experiences really belong to?

Were it not for this limitation of having a particular "duration," my experience would be simply experience — without personal pronoun. It would be the experience or "his-story" of entire mankind, reaching back into eternity. It is through the identification with a stretch of time, which means that I live from and through a limited range of experiences — which is my conditioning — that I have narrowed down my existence from the eternal to the ephemeral. This must be pretty clear to any objective student.

Now it is a fact of common experience that in deep sleep, in the split second after waking up, and also in the short intervals between successive thoughts or the satisfaction of different desires, there is a total absence of any feeling of "duration" and consequently of being a particular person. When the mind is totally relaxed in these conditions, there is no feeling of existence being progressive, no feeling of time. The feeling of duration is only assigned subsequent to the mind's relaxation, when once again thoughts start flowing. In the timeless state, there is purely a feeling of sentience, of pure Presence, not of any particular entity being present. It is then that one gets a forefeeling of one's real nature.

So it becomes clear that thought, which is always based on memory, is identical with time. But here again, just as in the case of space, we are drawn back into a self-affirming definition. The feeling of duration directs our attention to the body — which, after all is, all that can endure — but in itself this time awareness is purely dependent on memory. Memory is a cellular or bodily function, namely, the capacity of protoplasmic material to retain and store certain physicochemical changes in its substance, enabling it to function much like a tape recorder and play back certain engrams. This means then that to prove the soma's persistence in time, a somatic base is needed in the first place!

To sum up our findings, to prove the existence of the body-mind as a separate entity in space-time, we have had to postulate its very existence in the first place. One could even say it in a still simpler fashion: the proof of space-time existence requires a mind or "thought," but we cannot adduce the mind or thought process because it is thought itself that brings about separation between the "you" and the "me."

Working through such paradoxes, what is one left? One is left with an Emptiness, in which everything appears from moment to moment against a background of Infinity and Timelessness.

Thus, time or memory — the accumulation of "innate tendencies" or *vasanas* — is the basis of my present and future activities, for these are always grounded in the past. If I have no such knowledge, no such residue, activity will still take place but it will not be any action that is person-based. Understand well the enormous violence that is involved in the identification of the Infinite with an atom of space and the Eternal with an atom of time. This is the real origin of all violence, the existence of autonomous pseudo-entities called the "you" and the "me"; and there will never be a real end to this unless the primordial dualistic act is undone through true understanding of *advaitic* truth.

Moving from the theoretical to the practical, how does one test this, how does one act from one's real understanding? Let me give a simple example. Suppose I have a desire to start a new religion that I have invented for the betterment of mankind. Leaving out the question of whether I have really invented something fresh and viable — for that is not relevant here — the ordinary person will make vigorous efforts or even move heaven and earth to introduce his novel ideas that might make a difference in the world. In the course of carrying out his mission to save mankind, he may even make himself quite miserable.

Now the individual who has gone through a genuine spiritual transformation will equally set into motion certain activities to introduce his new religion or whatever it may be. But his actions will flow from a different source, a non-personal realm as solid as rock compared with which the base of personal choice is as soft as butter. In a sense, although others will not be able to see it that way, he has nothing to do with the introduction of the new religion. He will do the right things, but essentially he is not involved at all. It is as though he is not even present — the nearest thing to experiencing death while still in the body. In his vista, he will see that certain things need doing, but at least initially, any action will flow from a background of these unspoken questions: "Why should I — that is, this empirical manifestation in space-time — be involved, be doing anything? And, anyway, who is this entity who is doing the 'doing'?"

Thus, through such constant self-remembering, he is not putting himself out for any action, but action sucks him into itself, as it were. This is not a prescription for passivity or quietism; on the contrary — action will proceed and it will be immediate, without the slightest time interval — but the purity of the action is ever maintained. There is a "doing" without a "doer"; the *vasanas* are neutralized and the action emanates directly from the Emptiness, the source of everything that *is*. And like an arrow unfailingly hitting its target, the result will ever be most appropriate. Any serious *sadhaka* should always test himself operationally along such lines whenever a desire arises and, more generally, in any situation requiring action or a response of any kind. In this way, the ego, representing the unreal, will continually be held in check and beaten down by the real. One will then get a first-hand feeling for the freedom that awaits him who realizes his true Nothingness. This *sadhana* should be done consistently and persistently until it becomes as natural as breathing; falling short of that means it remains a mere intellectual or academic exercise.

Fully realizing *advaita*, which is one's real nature, assures that man is ever at peace with himself and violence remains unborn. Then where is any further need for "practicing nonviolence"?

No Such Thing as "Nothingness" or "Death" Can Ever Exist[1]

Regardless of superficial appearances and impressions, at no time is there an elimination or destruction of that which exists. In other words, at no time "nothing" comes into being. One might say therefore that ontologically the term "nothing" should be deleted from our working dictionary — which is exactly what the Greek philosopher Parmenides recommended when he stated: "You cannot know Non-Being, *nor even say it*." This conclusion may at first seem counterintuitive, yet even science points to the same truth through its mass-energy equivalence formula, $E = mc^2$, indicating that no thing ever truly disappears into "zero existence." If matter is "destroyed," it reappears as energy in the exact amount indicated by the formula, and vice versa. More generally, though the appearance of a thing — that is, its particular manifestation — may undergo various changes, yet what *is* — its underlying reality — remains ever the same.

Most people would say that surely at this point one has come upon the end of where logic can take us, but I

---

1 From a talk given at the *Inner Directions* Gathering in La Jolla, California, 1998.

would like to affirm here by stating that if one's original logical thesis is sound, one may be surprised to what extent the logical process may take one. (The great Indian sage, Sri Atmananda, even proved *advaita* by what he calls "the mathematical method"!; see *Rays of the Ultimate*, Publ. SAT, Santa Cruz, California.) Eventually a blending of the logical and the spiritual may take place, a transcendence of the intellectual process of discovery into one of direct perception or spiritual "in-seeing."

There is one further important inference to be made from the statement that there can be no such thing as "nothingness." It is that it voids the existence of "objects" and all separate entities. Because for the latter to be possible, they must have borders or delineations — either physical or psychological — that endow them with particular identities, allowing them to be individual objects and "beings."

Now what would separate the objects and entities from each other? Obviously, this could only be Nothingness. But having already seen the absolute nonexistence of Nothing or Nothingness, this invalidates the existence of objects as well as "persons." To maintain the existence of discrete persons there would have to exist something like a matrix of "nonentity" separating the postulated persons to give them personhood or individuality. In the absence of such a matrix of Nothingness, the "person" is a logical impossibility. In other words, it signals the end of dualism and affords clear evidence for non-dualism. Reality must therefore be considered to be one solid block, as it were. "Objects" as superficially perceived are only appearances, and there is no "I" as distinct from "you" and "he." Hence, all change is seen to be unreal, and space and time cease to have fundamental reality. Only the unchanging and indivisible is real. I am That, or more universally and accurately: "*We* are That, the Totality." Appearance-wise, one may assume and discard one or more bodies, and weave a web of thought around them just as we do in the dream state, but in reality, and to the truly Awakened, neither birth nor death exists, for That is immutable.

The Last Meditation: Reading the Book that is Oneself[1]

Many of us are highly knowledgeable in the sense of having read many books, attended many workshops in spirituality, yet we are not particularly literate when it comes to reading and understanding the book that is closest to ourselves, always available and which contains the deepest secrets of spirituality: the only book that is really worth reading, the book that is oneself. When I read this book with full attention, without distraction, I engage myself in a most supreme form of what I would like to call "the last meditation."

This last meditation ideally should be the first meditation, because the meditation I am referring to is truly final — one might say it is the meditation to end all meditations....And so, it can also be termed the only meditation that a human being needs to do. But not only am I using the term "final" in the strictly temporal sense, but also to indicate that my result or conclusion is of a qualitatively different nature than the conclusion or insight obtained in a

---

[1] Keynote address delivered at the *International Foundation for New Human Paradigms, Guadalajara, Mexico, November 20, 1998.*

187

strictly scientific or philosophical inquiry. For example, a scientist obtains a new insight into the nature of the physical world — let us say by discovering a more advanced theory of quantum mechanics or a more refined presentation of a holistic universe. What actually takes place is that he changes his outlook on his external reality, but in himself — his own being and functioning — he remains essentially unchanged. Also, the new images the scientist has acquired of the external world are not really final, although he is tempted to think so. Thus, this scientist-philosopher type of person may have an "aha experience" — sometimes called a "peak experience" — in which, in a single instant, his world perspective is fundamentally transformed, but in himself as the experiencer, he remains essentially unchanged. Since at this stage, his entire mental structure is based on thought, on concept, all this takes place within the field of the mind, and as long as the latter remains intact, there can be no total transformation involving his real being. On the other hand, in true transcendence, the experiencer himself disappears from the scene, and the subject is instantly transformed.

Thus, through the "final" meditation as referred to above, not only the world picture is changed beyond all recognition, but also the meditator himself is transformed; in fact, it would be more accurate to say he has disappeared from the scene. A characteristic of this metanoia is that there is no gradualism about it; that is, it is much like a switch, for it tends to operate from moment to moment. Another aspect is that no effort, no "thinking" per se, can accelerate one's spiritual emancipation; that is, a certain intangible element — call it "grace," if you like — appears indispensable. Finally, this opening up to reality initially takes place along very individual lines, but ultimately one observes certain identical, fundamental truths so well enunciated by such great Masters as Ramana Maharshi, Nisargadatta Maharaj and other *advaitic* sages. Where there are differences in the teaching, they are more differences in emphasis than in substance.

Traditionally, there are different types of meditation and as one of the highest forms of it, teachers have prompted us to meditate on the meditator, which comes down to asking the question "Who Am I?" Now my approach is just a tad different for a starting point, although in the end it comes down to the same thing. In first instance, I wish to investigate: How and what do I see, experience, what is "experience" to me and how do I gauge the world of my perception, my experience? Ultimately, I find that I inevitably arrive at that very same question: "Who or What Am I?" In first instance, "Who am I?" and then "What am I?" The difference between them is that "Who" still implies the nature of a person, whereas "What" goes beyond that and points to the impersonal.

Now first of all, during my entire waking life it can be stated that I experience — or more correctly, there is experience, since I don't actively do anything about it and leaving alone the fact that at this stage there is not too much clarity as to what is meant by the term "I." We are not talking here about experiences of a particular kind, those that I may want to elicit or manipulate and that have their origin in desire of one kind or another — or are induced by fear. Thus, in the present context, "experience" amounts to just another name for "being awake." Experience happens to me as long as I am not asleep or in a swoon.

Where does "experience" originate? That is obviously the next logical question to ask. The various sense impressions are coordinated and processed by the brain. Normally, the sense organs work in tandem with a corresponding part of the brain, except in dreams when it is the brain function only that is active, yet is capable of producing a "world" of sorts.

The prevailing view is that the sense organs are portals for experience to access us. Now I maintain that this is either only partly correct or totally false, depending upon one's point of view or the depth of understanding of self. When we use that term "portals," we obviously imply that something enters our being from the outside world. Now I maintain that on a deeper level, the outside and the inside world are one, and that this division is one purely projected within thought. "Outside" and "inside" are concepts based on the conventional view that we are our bodies, at least as far as our demarcation in space-time is concerned. And the accepted view has become so ingrained in the consciousness that it has become very difficult to eradicate. So I am trying to retrace my origin to the primordial condition in order to understand man's current predicament.

Essentially we are faced with a paradox, of the chicken and the egg variety. The basic confusion underlying our present state of understanding is the fact that the so-called "portals" are infinitely more than just conveyors of experience: they are actually the *generators* of experience. And this notwithstanding the often-repeated allegation that the sense organs themselves are innocent, as was so well stated by the late Alan Watts, and that corruption occurs only with the mind coming in. Broadly speaking, Watts is right, of course, but what is "the mind"? Within the present context should one declare this "mind" as a given? I feel that "thought" comes about as the result of a physiological stimulus in sensory perception, and that consequently the mind (selfhood or the sense of "I") springs into being as a result of the interaction of this germ of thought with Awareness or Consciousness. Isn't this what Sri Nisargadatta Maharaj admonished when he stated: Recede, recede! to trace the birth and primordial stirrings of the dualistic consciousness, of thought, from within the original purity of *advaita*? Let me quote you from his book *The Ultimate Medicine*:". . . the whole universe, everything that appears, is contained in the birth principle. This is the reason so much stress is placed on finding out what it is. Few people give attention to the birth principle, because they don't realize its importance. Because of the birth principle, everything is, the world is. All the knowledge of the world is contained in it. Only one in a crore (ten million) persons can find out what the birth principle is. And once you know it, everything, all knowledge, belongs to you — even liberation is yours." And in the *Gospel of Thomas*, Jesus, when asked by the disciples: "Tell us how our end will be," answered: "Have you discovered, then, the beginning that you look for the end? For where the beginning is, there the end will be. Blessed is he who will take his place in the beginning; he will know the end and will not experience death." [From the *Secret Sayings of Jesus* (also known as the *Gospel of Thomas*) No. 18, the manuscript unearthed at Hag Nammadi about half a century ago] It seems that Jesus is reminding his disciples to first learn their "Beginner's Zen," as it were, before speculating about the future, and that the new paradigm, which is apparently pointing towards the future, is in actual fact ever rooted in the understanding of the here-and-now.

Continuing our last meditation and germane to the present argument, I submit that within the primordial substratum, this layer of innocence, a subtle kind of duality is born, which, although it is on the physical level, makes possible, and in fact is essential to, the superimposition of a conceptual, emotional level. For example, the taste cells in the mouth come into contact with a sweet substance, such as honey. Immediately, there is sensation, pleasure is created, which then is seized upon by the mind with the thought: "I want more of that." And conversely, when the taste is bitter — or to take another example, there is a sudden, shrill and piercing noise — the body cells react in an opposite manner with an immediate recoil. Thus, before the mind has even realized the full depth of the experience, there has been a response from the body — usually with lightning speed. Then the mind comes in, with the realization "this is pleasant and I must have more of it," or "that is distasteful and I do not want it at all." As an aside, it must be stated here that all this is strongly related to the mystery of the Creation of the World, which is not an event in time and space and is neither individual nor collective but occurs at every manifestation of Awareness. When I came into the world, strangely, the world came into being with me, and upon my death I do not leave the world but the world leaves with me; just like each time I dream, I enter and leave a different world inhabited by different people. This observation forms the cornerstone of the *Advaitic* insight and outlook, which has been so well expounded in all its various aspects by Ramana Maharshi.

The next step in our investigation is to realize that duality on the physical plane necessarily occurs before there can be any question of duality in the psychological sense. Desire and fear occur naturally with the awareness of a physical world. Just as physiologically the continuity of biological life and its maintenance are predicated upon the divisibility of the cell unit, so the life of the psyche is preconditioned by the functional duality of the sense organs. It is within this context that their nature as generators of experience must be understood.

Coming now to the crux of the matter, the following situation can then be seen to prevail: To explain the existence of the physical world, and my somatic being in particular, I need the presence of a body in the first place. This is the essential modus operandi: To see, to experience anything, I need sense organs. So to become aware of my so-called "body," I need its sensors. But what are they? They are obviously themselves of the nature of "body." Thus, it now reads as follows: to become aware of my body, I need my body in the first place — my body comes into view, into being, by being there in the first place. An obvious tautology! A short time after this remarkable situation had fully dawned upon me, I chanced upon the following words by the famous South Indian sage, Krishna Menon, also known as Sri Atmananda: "Each sense organ perceives only itself; knowledge knows only knowledge, and love loves only love. In short, the instrument utilized is itself perceived by the instrument." Atmananda, in further confirmation, said: "A thing can prove the existence of nothing other than itself. Sensations can prove the existence of sensations alone. So you can also prove only yourself." (By which, he meant, of course, that there never is any independent evidence of a creature's existence.) This signifies then that experience is a closed system, or as we had phrased it: the sense organs are indeed generators and not mere portholes! Oddly, they are simultaneously generators and sensors. In other words, the body exists only to itself, but other than that has no objective existence at all! One simply has been hypnotized, duped into accepting its phony existence for real. We now understand the body to be like the rainbow in the sky, deceptively real yet only a misunderstanding by the senses. And just as nobody would identify with this or any other mere "appearance," so no sane person should identify any longer with the body. Hence, if one is not the body, then one is That which realizes the situation thusly, in other words, the Awareness or the Consciousness — one's true and only Self (or *Atman*, as it is called in the East).

Outcome of the Process

To recapitulate, through discovery of the original split in our perception, we have rediscovered and regained our original Wholeness, which is the Consciousness. Our meditation has made it clear that there is no such thing as a physical body in the first place, whether "my own body"or "others' bodies," these are all ideas only — words, thoughts, concepts — without underlying physical reality. And even these last two words are part of the faulty way of seeing and digesting our experience. The realization that experiences are self-wrought, and that there are only these impressions without any physical basis — in fact, that any physical basis itself is nonexistent — has a tremendous effect on one's world view and by implication, one's functioning. Far from the soma being the Ground from which all intelligent life springs, it is the soma that springs forth from that Ground of Beingness. And if that which is designated as "body" has no real (i.e., independent) existence, nor the mind resting somehow on that mythical unit, then all the ideas of living and dying are part of our fantasy world. Ramana Maharshi ever denied independent existence to body-mind: "The body is the result of thoughts" and "The seer sees the mind and the senses as within the Self and not as apart from it." Not only does it become clear that there is neither "a body" nor "a mind," but only some vague something, an empirical entity — one hesitates to call it "reality"— that may be designated as "body-mind." Yet it is this false "ego" that has led one by the nose for all this time, some ghostlike entity that, as Ramana Maharshi defined it so well, has arisen from the interaction of Consciousness with "body." Thus, all that we have been thinking and philosophizing about is now seen as just so much piffle in the wind.

Life and death so-called are now seen in an entirely different light: neither exists as such. They only appear to be. Since in the past I had accepted the existence of my body for real, I now realize that I have accepted its reality on the evidence of itself only — as if it were a foregone conclusion. Not only is that definitely impermissable in the realm of logic, but it is also a piece of loaded evidence of the kind that Ramana Maharshi referred to as the policeman catching the thief who is himself. Consequently, living and dying are seen to be part of the old ignorance: what appeared to be my final destination — death of body and self — is seen to be a mere juggling of words or ideations. Only the Consciousness or Awareness is real and only That I am. My only function is that of Witnessing — which is really only another word for Awareness (but don't be misled by the grammatical structure of the language to think there is an associated "witness").

These newly acquired insights have various implications that are far-reaching, in more ways than one. First of all, with respect to my self, there no longer is an "inside" and an "outside." The Universe which one had imagined being out there, is not really out there at all. "Out there" implies a physical reality outside the observation platform that I call "my body" or my sensory apparatus. And we have just discovered that there is absolutely nothing of the kind outside that apparatus and that even this apparatus is a only a mental projection devoid of materiality, since space-time itself is a mere mental construct. Thus, although we may be talking, for example, about traveling into deep space on a spaceship, both that spaceship and the physical universe in which the travel takes place are actually contained within the mental field that is the "me" and derive their existence from it. Other than being mental constructs or concepts, they have no reality. Ramana Maharshi puts it succinctly as follows: *"The objective world is really subjective. An astronomer discovers a new star at immeasurable distance and announces that its light takes thousands of years to reach the earth. Well, where is the star in fact? Is it not in the observer? But people wonder how a huge globe, larger than the Sun, at such a distance can be contained in the brain cells of a man. The space, the magnitudes and the paradox are all in the mind only."* [emphasis mine] Similarly it is with my sense of time, of "becoming," which governs all our activities. Time, like space, is a fiction and my existence is only the ever-present Now — we cannot even say it lies within the ever-present Now because that still suggests some materiality. Once I give up the entire physical and mental field, such as in deep sleep or true Self-Realization, there is absolutely nothing to disturb one — nothing that the mind can get a grip on.

One then lives in a Universe that is neither physical nor mental yet is much more than the sum total of both. It is our eternal home, our real Being and may therefore legitimately be called the Self, but there is in fact no term that can adequately define it. That is why it is imperative for each of us to undertake this final meditation for ourselves. My Self is ever existent and has no particular place within any scheme of things because it is all that exists and carries everything within itSelf — all that ever is, has been or will be.

When what is consensually called "death" appears, I see a "body" disappear from view — as part of an unending array of "bodies" appearing and disappearing, just like the waves of the ocean — but nothing more can and needs to be said.

Realizing the profound truth of all this cannot fail to have an immense effect on one's being and functioning. There can be no more talk about theory and practice: truly seeing one's reality brings to a stop the many habitual ideations and actions. This is because the driving force behind the activities has evaporated! The millions of things that up to now had caused us to feel hot under the collar have suddenly lost their appeal, either positively or negatively, and as time goes by there takes place a gradual emptying out of psychological memory. Up to this point, one had been in the grip of the mind — the mind that continually creates a nonexistent world, one of essentially self-created desires and self-created fears, and which is literally unstoppable in its endeavor.

One becomes acutely aware of the statement by the Buddha, allegedly the first words spoken after his enlightenment experience: "Desire, I know thy root, from imagination art thou born; no more shall I indulge in imagination. I shall have no desire anymore." And what did the Buddha in this connection mean by "imagination"? The erroneous idea that one is nothing more nor less than that constantly changing shape vaguely identified as "the body" — which is the primary act of our false identification. Jesus Christ also clearly and beautifully refers to the state of purity before sense perception and mind origination have extracted their toll: "I shall give you what no eye has seen and what no ear has heard and what no hand touched *and what has never occurred to the human mind.*" (*Thomas*, 17). [emphasis mine]

You may note his clear reference here to the transcendence of the main senses of seeing, hearing and touch, and climaxed by transcendence of the very mind itself, leading to the state Ramana Maharshi refers to as *jagrat-sushupti* or wakeful sleep (perhaps one might also refer to it as a state of unconscious Awareness, that is, pure awareness without thought, as in the intervals between two thoughts).

In the same vein, the Zen Master Lin-chi made a statement that sounds remarkably similar to that of Jesus: "How to call this very distinct thing, this solitary light that has never been incomplete, but that the eye does not see, the ear does not hear? An ancient one once said: 'To say that it is a thing, is to miss the target.'"

A more extensive, but equally clear treatment of the subject is given in the Upanishads: "That not seen by the eyes, but by which the eyes see: know that That is indeed Brahman — not what is being worshipped here." And "That not heard by the ear, but by which the ear hears: know that That indeed is Brahman — not what is being worshipped here" (*Kena Upanishad* 1-7 and 8).

Finally, *Ribu Gita* (Chapter 5, Verse 11) sums it all up neatly: "The organs of knowledge, the senses, the organs of action, waking, dream, deep sleep, and any other such state are all like the horns of a hare" — which is a cute way of saying they don't actually exist. Isn't it a marvelous surprise to find Jesus, a famous Zen Master, the Upanishads, and the *Ribu Gita* all under the same banner, as it were!

By now it must have become abundantly clear that all that mind emanation of ours is totally invalid. The mind recognizes its own limitations and basic impotence, and by virtue of that recognition spontaneously switches off. There is a realization that one is not body, mind nor senses, but the Consciousness or the Absolute, which itself cannot be defined because everything else is defined by It and if it were to be defined, it could only be defined by the mind which is subsidiary to That. So just rest in the Consciousness, but don't even know you are resting in that Consciousness, because then you are back in the mind and you have switched out again. If one can do this, even for a moment, a strange calm or feeling of overwhelming bliss, freedom and quietude takes place mysteriously; and even if that is all there is, who would, and who is there left, to complain? It is summed up tersely in the *Ribu Gita* (Chapter 3, Verse 44) as follows: "There is no bondage, but only Consciousness. There is then no 'Liberation,' but only Consciousness. Just Consciousness is the only Reality. This is the Truth — the Truth — I say in the name of Siva." It is a tremendous discovery for each of us to make — and therefore truly, the last meditation, with the only subsequent challenge to remain forever awake.[2]

---

[2] Quotations from Ramana Maharshi are from *Talks with Ramana Maharshi* (publ. Inner Directions Foundation, Carlsbad, California, 2000); from Sri Atmananda are from *Spiritual Discourses of Sree Atmananda*, Part II, 1953-1959.

Man is Caught in a Web of His Own Making[1]

In the search towards self-understanding, the body is both a facilitator — a natural and necessary starting point — and a roadblock. The body, being our most familiar item, is the most taken for granted; yet without it, nothing else would exist! As a facilitator, where else would one begin? It is the perception by the body that leads to everything else. Literally, through the body, the whole world comes into view. Without body, there would be absolutely nothing, nothing to be perceived and nothing by which to perceive; in other words, there would be no world, no mind and no consciousness — for all these come into existence only through the body. I am not saying that there would be nothing, a pure emptiness, devoid of existence, but body is the instrument that enables one to get a handle on the world, to utter "I" and to initiate any mind activity whatsoever.

As a roadblock, it is the great misleader, for its apparent solidity lends its some authority with a science-impressed civilization. And since we have taken body as our starting point in any activity, and anything at all is

---

[1] Subject of a Workshop given at the *7th International Conference of the New Paradigms "Holistic Vision for the 21st Century,"* November 17-21, 1999, Guadalajara, Mexico.

viewed in relation to that very body, there never is any investigation as to how the world literally comes into being as the result of its activity.

The most common and seductive argument for the apparent reality of duality — that is, the world of space and time — is that we perceive and experience it thusly. Well, at one time it was our common-sense perception that the earth was the center of the Universe because it appeared that the sun was moving around the earth. Also, matter was thought to be a continuous, solid medium, until science figured out that it consisted largely of empty space and that even the particles in it were not like solid little tennis balls but something much more ethereal.

Essentially, we have accepted space-time on the basis of the common perception that when our eyes are open, "objects" — which presuppose space-time — are perceived (as contained) in it; and these objects are not perceived when our eyes are closed. But when we are asleep and dreaming our eyes are closed and yet we perceive objects and on waking realize that these objects do not (and did not) really exist. The important lesson here is that the simple test of perceiving "objects" does not really prove their existence, and therefore the reality of space-time. Similarly, when waking from the dream of our present existence into Self-realization, there is the profound discovery that the world of space-time objects, which includes my own body, is a dream; and that a mind built upon the basis of an individual "entity" is equally an erroneous concept.

When we use the term "I" in any statement, what do we actually mean in this connection? The "I" is obviously a concept which is based, in first instance, on the body, on the idea of possessing and being a distinct physical form with practically imperceptible day-to-day change; otherwise, to talk about a "me" would obviously have little mean-

ing, unless it was meant as referring to the collective. Once
this concept was accepted, we developed the idea of the
(individual) mind, as a separate psychological entity deriving from this "I." But what is the concrete evidence for both
assumptions? Now first of all, what is the evidence that I
indeed occupy a piece of space designated by the term
"body"? The only evidence for this is the information pro-
vided by my senses, that is, *the sense organs*, which themselves are part of that mythical entity called "body" and
exactly that which is to be proved as existing in the first
place. In other words, all I can come up with is a circular
argument or "begging the question," as the saying goes.
Thus, "I," individual body and individual mind are ultimately all nonexistent.

Another approach to my alleged separate individuality is the question of my continuity in time. Like space, I
must discover whether there is such a thing as time at all.
In first instance, I must further learn about myself. I need to
trace my origin, the very earliest sign of when this particular "I" came into being — the transition point, or the inter-
section, of nothingness and thingness or beingness. That, I
feel, would represent my true birth. Exploring this avenue,
one will soon come to the discovery that it is impossible to
identify such a beginning of the "I." It is really impossible to
say when that "I" began, nor can I say when that "I" will end.
I can fairly assume my inability to identify any point of termination of the "I," for at the point of shedding the body
through illness or incapacity, the entity that could possibly
tell me about its ending will already have left or been
silenced. Thus, I am not and cannot be aware of any death
anymore than I can be aware of birth of the "I."

I have now come to realize the fallacy of our usual
approach to the problem. We start to investigate our temporal nature by examining first of all an historical entity, on

the basis of an assumption defined by its birth at a certain date and demise at an uncertain time in the future. But we are not allowed to do so, for this is exactly what is yet to be proved — the existence and definition of the "I" within time. So once again we have been begging the question. My final conclusion must be that the "I" is not in time at all, and since time had been predicated upon a fixed temporal nature of the "I," there can be no justification for projecting an absolute space-time framework on the world at large. Thus, time — like space — has no absolute existence but is relative; that is, it is a projection from the mind. Only the Self that transcends both space and time is real.

The sum total of the newly acquired insights can only mean the complete eradication of the dualistic worldview. Since, in actuality, there are no individual bodies, or separate entities in any shape or form, everything based on that assumption collapses. And, logically, the same must go for the assumed separate spheres of the mind: there is only thought or Mind, and the imagined separate or individual thinker is also part of the illusory spectacle.

Hence, in the Upanishads it is written:

That not thought by mind,
but by which, they say, mind is thought:
know that That indeed is Brahman — not what they
worship here. (*Kena*, 1-6)

I know all this goes against common sense, but that common sense is largely a habit, that of seeing things for aeons in a particular way, without realizing the initial error of our observation/interpretation. One does not have to be of a particularly spiritual or religious disposition to see the error of our observation: the gross way of "begging the question" with respect to the actual, fundamental nature of our physical form and the consequent postulation of an individual mind. And just as one wakes up from a dream and the seeing therein of all kinds of entities that are subsequently found to be nonexistent in the waking state, so also *one wakes up from the dream of inaccurate observation* and superficial interpretation of the evidence of our senses into a reality which is free from all divisions. One is what one has always been and always remains: Pure Awareness only, or the one and only Self without divisions.

Epilogue

Unfortunately, there exists a widely misunderstood idea with those who have been following the foregoing treatises in predominantly theoretical fashion. They think that their realization — or what they take for realization — can in some way be expressed semantically, preferably in glowing terms of experiential or philosophical wisdom. They thereby miss the whole point that realization means the end of all conceptualization, in other words, the total silencing of the mind. For, when the mind has been fully neutralized, how can there still be any conceptualization, any ideas, any words? There obviously cannot, only silence must prevail — a silence which is not contrived or imposed. This therefore is the real touchstone for one's transformation. In this way, one has arrived at the logical and natural outcome of the sequential process of meditation which began with the examination of our sensory perception, turning in on itself and finally destroying itself, until Nothing (that is, on a different level, everything) remains. And so, it is an absolute impossibility to express that state in any way at all, for there is no mind, no thought, no concept available that would be required for its articulation.

Letting go of the Mind

To gain some further perspective into this matter of man's innate condition, let us consider the two terminal points of "birth" and "death" in a human's history, which may give us some clue about the nature of what we really are, which we call "I" or "me."

Upon entering this world, we do so carrying as yet no concepts, no thoughts and no burden of time, or memory, because although there have been experiences, these have been physiological and not psychological in nature. There are physiological wants but as yet no psychological wants or desires. As time goes by, and memory becomes more expansive, the whole machinery of thoughts, desires, and "individuality" develops and finally one may talk of a "person" in the psychological sense. Not only has one entered the world but, more appropriately and accurately, the world has entered one's being, the empirical individual. Although the condition does not last long in terms of man's usual life span, each of us starts life as an automaton. Then, with the developing brain and establishment of psychological memory, leading to the thirst for experiences as desire and its opposite as fear, thoughts and concepts take a hold and henceforth dominate our being until death or realization occurs (and the latter is actually a form of death).

When we leave this world, we do so as we entered it, a *tabula rasa* because we let go of everything. More accurately, the world leaves: it leaves us alone, or rather all One, that is, without any divisions. Nothing is anymore within our control, but more importantly, there is nothing anymore to control. There is the same total let-go as when entering deep sleep. Except this time it is for good, for real, and if there is a renewal of the show, we have to start from scratch. Within this interval, we did acquire millions of concepts as ideas, thoughts, fears and desires and it is through these that our life was a tug of war between short-lived joys and sufferings, with nary a moment of tranquility.

In between these points of birth and death, all unhappiness is seen to take place. Also, the joy, but this joy was basically the opposite of unhappiness and not the Happiness that lies beyond all pairs of opposites, and which is concomitant on liberation of the dualistic consciousness.

In conclusion, it seems clear then that psychological suffering arises and manifests exclusively with and through thought and concept — in other words, whenever a mind is active. And it appears equally evident that bliss prevails when the mind is in abeyance and absolute silence prevails. All thoughts, all concepts, notions about there being a "self," "God," philosophy, scriptures, etc., all that has disappeared and is seen to be artificial — man-made and mind-made and not reality. The death of the mind has brought a unique Silence. Then one truly is beyond the intellect; beyond theology, philosophy, *advaita* versus *dvaita* — beyond all knowledge, because one is prior to thought and memory. That Silence, however, is not a mere absence of noise; it is the very source of Creation, from which all opposites arise and into which they again disappear. It will always remain a mystery to the little mind.

Having come to the end of the road by means of this final meditation — the end of all mind activity and the end of reason and logic — what more is there to say or do? Obviously, nothing — since all such sayings and doings are mind activities. And all mental activities, whether the most "sublime" or the most "base," are within the field of limitation and unreality. But what is interesting — most interesting — is what takes place or does not take place, when the mind has ceased its nefarious activities and is in a state of total abstention.

Because the aforementioned state is so unfamiliar to most of us, we are inclined to put labels to it and equate it with all sorts of "isms." For instance, some might say and are saying that what is being described, or even advocated, is Nihilism, or — equally shocking! — Atheism. Nihilism is the idea that nothing ever exists, a total negation or destruction of all that we can imagine, all that we have cherished. The mistake here is that we are not dealing with true opposites. At this point, opposites no longer exist. Opposites exist only within the mind or on the conceptual level. This is the meaning of true transcendence, and we are not allowed to mix levels!

The situation reminds me somewhat — but only by way of analogy — of when in learning algebra as a child, I first learned of the existence of negative numbers. I could understand +2, but what about −2? How could this be real? To facilitate understanding, I was told that when +2 means possession of two items of whatever, −2 means its opposite, that I owe someone 2 units. Thus, I became habituated to mixing positive and negative numbers and manipulating these as I wished. But it was only much later that I had to confront the meaning of zero, when I found I could not and was not allowed to manipulate zero in the same way I did positive and negative numbers. Thus multiplying or dividing by zero was on a distinctly different level than multiplying by 1, 2, etc.; it was totally meaningless and, in fact, mathematically unsound and prohibited. I finally realized that the true opposite of +2 was not −2, but zero, and perhaps also Infinity — since the same strangeness associated with zero was found to exist in connection with that concept designated by the name of "Infinity."

In the same way, existence and nonexistence, life and death, theism and atheism, "effort" and "non-effort," have meaning only on the mind level. All such discussion becomes meaningless or non-valid upon transcendence of this level; one then is truly Beyond Religion.

Lights of Grace Catalog

from

The Blue Dove Foundation

The Blue Dove Foundation is a non-profit, tax-exempt organization and not affiliated with any particular path, tradition, or religion. Our mission is to deepen the spiritual life of all by making available works on the lives, messages, and examples of saints and sages of all religions and traditions, as well as other spiritual titles that provide tools for inner growth.

The Blue Dove Foundation supports the publication of inspirational books and tapes from Blue Dove Press. The foundation also distributes important spiritual works of other publishers, including hundreds of titles from India, through our web site and *Lights of Grace* catalog.

From Saint Teresa of Avila, to Sri Ramana Maharshi, to Milarepa, the Tibetan yogi—from *The Koran*, to *The Zohar*, to *The Mahabharata*—we have assembled an inspired collection of spiritual works at its most diverse and best.

For a free Catalog contact:

The Blue Dove Foundation
4204 Sorrento Valley Blvd. Suite K
San Diego, CA 92121
Phone: (858)623-3330 FAX: (858)623-3325
Orders: (800)691-1008
e-mail: bdp@bluedove.org
Web site: www.bluedove.org